A RAMBLE AMONG THE
MUSICIANS OF GERMANY

Da Capo Press Music Reprint Series

GENERAL EDITOR

FREDERICK FREEDMAN

VASSAR COLLEGE

A RAMBLE AMONG THE
MUSICIANS OF GERMANY

By Edward Holmes

New Introduction and Indexes by
CHARLES CUDWORTH
Cambridge University

 DA CAPO PRESS • NEW YORK • 1969

A Da Capo Press Reprint Edition

ML
423
.H75

This Da Capo Press edition of *A Ramble Among the Musicians
of Germany* is an unabridged republication of the first edition
published in London in 1828 as the work of an anonymous
"Musical Professor."

Library of Congress Catalog Card Number 68-16239

Copyright © 1969 by Da Capo Press
A Division of Plenum Publishing Corporation
227 West 17th Street
New York, N. Y. 10011

CONTENTS

INTRODUCTION

———

THIS charming and unpretentious little book of musical travels was published anonymously in 1828 as the work of "A musical professor" — that's to say, not a professor of music, as we might be tempted to think, but a professional musician. The writer was in fact Edward Holmes, later famous as the author of the first full-length English biography of Mozart.

Holmes was a distinguished figure in the musical and literary world of early nineteenth-century London. He was born about 1797, probably in or near London, and was educated at the celebrated academy of John Clarke at Enfield in Middlesex. There he became friendly with John Keats and Charles Cowden-Clarke, and first began to imbibe a taste for literature and music. On leaving school he was apprenticed to a bookseller, but later forsook the trade for music. He studied music with Vincent Novello (founder of the famous publishing firm) and for some time lived in Novello's house in what is now Oxford Street, where he made friends with many famous people, in-

cluding Leigh Hunt, Charles Lamb, Percy Bysshe
Shelley, John Cramer, Thomas Attwood, Johann
Nepomuk Hummel, Felix Mendelssohn, and Franz
Liszt.

When the newspaper, the *Atlas*, was founded in
1826, Holmes "undertook the department devoted to
musical criticism" and there made quite a name for
himself as a music critic with a fine literary style. It
was in 1827 that he set off on the continental tour
which eventually led to the publication of the present
book, and although one would never guess it from
the text, he had with him a female companion in the
matronly form of Mary Novello, Vincent's wife.
Together they visited, among other places, Antwerp,
Cologne, Munich, Vienna, Leipzig, Dresden, and
Berlin, sailed hazardously down the Danube on an
immense raft, just as Dr. Charles Burney had done
half a century before, and suffered the privations, as
well as the pleasures, of prerailway continental travel.

Nothing daunted, Mary set out again the next year,
this time with her husband, to visit Mozart's widow
and aged sister in Salzburg; the story of her journey
can be read in Nerina Medici and Rosemary Hughes'
A Mozart Pilgrimage (London, Novello, 1955).
Meanwhile Holmes brought out the *Ramble* anony-

mously — an open secret which was admitted in print years later in his obituary in the *Musical Times* for October 1, 1859.

But to return to Holmes' increasingly busy professional life: From 1833 onwards, he was organist of All Saints' Church, Poplar, and later of Holloway Chapel. He was also in considerable demand as a fashionable piano teacher and as a writer on musical matters. Besides serving as critic of the *Atlas*, he wrote in *Fraser's Magazine* and the *Spectator*, and when Vincent Novello's son, J. Alfred Novello, founded the *Musical Times* in 1844, Holmes proceeded to pepare for it some of his best articles, writing on Mozart, Purcell, and Blow, among others. In 1845 he published his classic *Life of Mozart*, and three years later wrote an enthusiastic review, in the *Atlas*, of Berlioz's first London concert, thereby making a firm friend of the great French composer, who referred to him as one of London's leading music critics and described the *Life of Mozart* as "much admired."

Holmes is said to have visited America in the late 1840's, but little is known of his visit, if indeed it occurred; in any case he was back in London in the early fifties, when he served on the committee for

Berlioz's ill-fated "testimonial concert," which failed to take place in July, 1853.

At fifty-odd, Holmes must have seemed a completely confirmed bachelor (although there were rumors of earlier flirtations with Shelley's widow and sister), but in 1857 he suddenly surprised everyone by marrying Louisa Webbe, granddaughter of the celebrated glee composer, Samuel Webbe. However Holmes had only two years of marital happiness before he died "of a ten days' illness" on August 28, 1859, at his house in Albert Street, Regent's Park, London, and not, as so often is erroneously stated, in the U.S.A.

Holmes left behind a great many admirable periodical articles and two excellent books. One, the famous *Life of Mozart,* is a classic of its kind and still well worth reading in spite of the vast amount of Mozartian research since its publication. The second book is the present *Ramble Among the Musicians of Germany,* which deserves to be much better known. Besides being full of information, it is charmingly written, with gentle humour and a quiet irony, all very typical of Holmes' general character.

It is interesting to note how the musical center of gravity had changed in the half century between Dr.

Burney's travels and those of Holmes. Burney had passed through Germany on his way to his own musical Mecca, Italy; Holmes deliberately sought out Germany, with Vienna as the very center of music-making for his day. In the main, his idealization of German music was justified, although even Germany let him down musically at times. The organist he heard in Cologne Cathedral was "extremely bad . . . ; his interludes between the Gregorian tones amazed me, from their unreligious and anomalous mixture of the music of a ballet or tea-garden with the cloistral severity of the chant." At Frankfurt he was disappointed by the acoustics of the theater, since "the violins seem[ed] to be always *con sordini*." In a Lutheran church at Darmstadt he discovered that even Germans "*may* and *can* sing out of tune." And although, as an early Romantic, he was ready to rhapsodize about the Rhineland, his eulogy has a characteristic little sting in its tail: "The country is so romantic that one would be transported back to the age of chivalry, except for that vile modern necessity of settling one's bill. . . ." *Tafelmusik* annoyed him: "Music is too heavenly an art to be degraded into mere sauce." At Berlin he commented wrily on Spontini, who was rewarded with "about 600*l*. [£]

a-year for manufacturing an opera occasionally," but he was delighted to encounter in W.F.E. Bach "a scion of the illustrious stock of Sebastian." Among his many illuminating comments is the remark that in Germany the organs were so huge and heavy in action that "an organist should have the bodily thews of a porter." A "lady performer (unless she were of Amazonian stock) would be a phenomenon."

Holmes is very quotable indeed, with a flair for pithy bon mots such as "Port wine has spoiled much music, has led to much inefficient fingering, and many wrong chords." On one sempiternal subject, the behavior of prima donnas, he writes: "Many a time has the poor conductor . . . had his head hammered with a thick score, for not being sufficiently prompt in his obedience." He attended many concerts on his tour, heard a number of operas, witnessed many masses and services (both high and low, Lutheran and Roman), talked with countless musicians, argued with coachmen and raftsmen and diligence drivers, and generally enjoyed himself one way or another, except perhaps in the alleys of Imperial Vienna, where a "detestable stench is continually reminding an Englishman of the peculiarity in his conformation, a nose that discriminates." His picture of musical life in early nineteenth-century *Mitteleuropa* is of immense interest to any musical historian, yet at the same time his general comments on men and manners are so lively and so acutely observed that his little book goes far toward anticipating George Bernard Shaw's claim that he could write about music in such a way that it would interest the tone-deaf.

So, homage to Holmes; and the best way to render him homage is to follow him as he goes on his highly agreeable and entertaining *Ramble Among the Musicians of Germany*.

Cambridge University   CHARLES CUDWORTH
January 1968

A RAMBLE

AMONG

THE MUSICIANS OF GERMANY.

A RAMBLE

AMONG

THE MUSICIANS OF GERMANY,

GIVING SOME

ACCOUNT OF THE

OPERAS OF MUNICH, DRESDEN, BERLIN, &c.

WITH REMARKS UPON

THE CHURCH MUSIC, SINGERS, PERFORMERS,
AND COMPOSERS;

AND A

SAMPLE OF THE PLEASURES AND INCONVENIENCES THAT AWAIT
THE LOVER OF ART ON A SIMILAR EXCURSION.

BY A MUSICAL PROFESSOR.

LONDON :

PUBLISHED BY HUNT AND CLARKE,
YORK STREET, COVENT GARDEN.

1828.

PREFACE.

As the preface to a little book of this kind will de-
note what Shakespear calls " a foregone conclusion," and appear to the reader like the summing
up of the judge, and the verdict of the jury, before
the cause is tried, I must beg that (unless he be
of unusual faith and trustingness) he withhold
his concurrence with the opinions here expressed
of German music and professors until he has read
the following account of the writer's experiences
in an expedition undertaken last summer to see
what Germany now produces in the art. If he
doubts then, he must travel and hear for himself.
My principal aim in this place is to bespeak the
good nature of the reader; for though I have not
attempted to write dissertations on the natural
history and statistics of Germany, nor to discuss
matters of religion or politics, nor to give a guide
to curiosities, I have chosen not to shut my eyes

to other matters besides the main object of my journey, principally to make it *readable* by those who are not exclusively amateurs of the art, and that the musical discussion of the volume might not run into the tiresome. What was chiefly wanted in this country was, that German music and performers should be heard with English ears; for the accounts which reach England through their magazines and journals of musical performances, being written by those who are " native there and to the manner born," necessarily want much of that interest which may be found in those of a fresher observer.

The admiration of German taste in the science has produced in some a ludicrous exaggeration of respect towards people who have no claim to it ; so much so, that the mere use of the language has spread a charm over the sugar-bakers and tailors of the metropolis ; and like the little boy who took it for a certainty that music which contained a great many flats and sharps must be good, the authority of one born in Mozart's country, and speaking like him, would scarce be questioned.

Whoever wishes to see Germany in its beauty, and its people at their best, must get beyond Düsseldorf and the Rhine, and proceed towards the south. Here he shall find, by five o'clock of a summer's afternoon, the houses clear of inhabitants; music, the theatres, parties of friends who meet to enjoy the society of one another in the open air, are the constant engagements of the public. Nor are sacred feast-days wanting, on which the most pious abjuration of work is enjoined and practised, and where it would be thought one of the deadliest of sins not to seek out that kind of enjoyment most agreeable.

Music is so much more extensively cultivated in Germany than in England, that though one may find no band equal to that of the Philharmonic Society, fifty may be found only inferior to it: and then the object which the foreign artist proposes to himself in the exercise of his profession being the love of the thing itself, instead of emolument, the spirit of a performance comes out better among them, if the letter of it is not given in so masterly a manner as here. In their singers and wind in-

strument players (always excepting certain individuals) they are decidedly our superiors; but in
their violin school they appear to me inferior both
to England and France. As for the audiences at
the opera-houses and concerts, they ever manifest a
most laudable desire to be improved, and do not
begin to grow impatient in a new composition the
instant they lose sight of a prominent melody; this
gives the composer a better chance of being understood; add to which, that every individual performer
being pretty well skilled in the theory, there are
vocal pieces executed with ease in Germany which
might not be attempted here while the present imperfect knowledge of harmony is tolerated in stage-
favourites. There is at present a great deal of
vocal talent in Germany; and I have never heard
a single chorus of an opera or oratorio there which
did not go with great precision as to time, and perfectly in tune.

With respect to other matters foreign to music to
be found in this volume, it is hoped that the playful
tone taken in the narrations of some of them may
form no objection to the serious intention of the

whole; and in defence of this plan, let it be chari-
tably remembered, that with cheerful weather, a
lovely country, cordial friends, and good Rhine-
wine, it would be difficult to be didactic. Whatever is here described, however imperfectly, has
actually been seen, a fact which former tourists have
now rendered it necessary to avouch, for it is a
curious coincidence that Charles Campbell, Esq.
and Dr. Render were so similarly impressed with
the view of Manheim, that they have described it
in precisely the same words. Since the voyage of
discovery made by Dr. Burney in search of the
origin of counterpoint, we have received no account of the occupations and mode of living
among German artists, nor any comparison of
their excellencies or defects with those of our
own. I can say nothing stronger in praise of
Germany than that I long to revisit it; and that
the recollection of the time spent with friends at
Munich, on the Danube, Prague, and other
places, is to me as a fine dream to turn to, when
bad weather or perverse accidents make English
existence a little monotonous. As for the na-

tional character, it is but little understood in
England; and it might appear romantic if I
were to say all that occurs to me upon it; besides, I have been bribed by too much music
and friendliness to be strictly impartial on such
a subject: but I can advise all lovers of the arts
who wish to enjoy a holiday of mind and body,
and to indulge in " mirth, that after no repenting
draws," to make trial of Germany.

A RAMBLE

AMONG

THE MUSICIANS OF GERMANY.

James Whiting, Printer, Beaufort House, Strand.

A SUMMER

AMONG

MUSIC AND MUSICAL PROFESSORS

IN GERMANY.

ANTWERP.

If the reader be one who finds variety and satisfaction in church music, if with the masses of Haydn
and Mozart, with paintings and architecture, he be
content to eschew theatrical amusements, this place
will give him pleasure. Antwerp is especially a
religious city, that is, after the continental fashion,
where religion is unmixed with gloom, and cer-
monies and observances serve as playthings for the
inhabitants—ever giving them something to stare at
and talk about; and where they keep up the ball
very pleasantly between the excitement of sinning
and the amusement of shriving. For the English
musician it is however a sort of Utopia. No temporal
business interferes to stop the daily performance of
that class of music which in our Protestant country
is eagerly sought after by amateurs in the various
holes and corners of our metropolis which furnish

Catholic chapels—places in which the imagination can but ill conceive the pompous celebration of the mass as it takes place in the vast churches of the continent, where music, painting, and architecture blending together, form, like colours when combined, another material, and produce in the mind poetry. I can give but a faint idea of the sweet half-monastic life one leads in Antwerp, it would be as impossible there to neglect attendance at matins, nones, or vespers, as if one had for years taken the vows of St. Francis or St. Dominic; and the magnificent tower of the cathedral, which stands out most majestically from the Scheld, is ever and anon sending forth with its deep-toned heavy bell, some "note of preparation," some warning of duties to be fulfilled. Indeed, without entering the churches, the critical musical faculty is provoked every quarter of an hour by a profane march, which the carillons in the tower of the cathedral never fail to perform, I suppose for the amusement of the numerous jack-daws who have there found "their coign of 'vantage," and who, though out of the pale of the church, and without benefit of clergy, might be treated with something a little better in tune. The hideously inharmonious jangling of these bells, the lamentable attempt at harmonizing a melody, infuses a spirit into the heels somewhat at variance with the tranquillity with which one would otherwise loiter round this old and honourable city: and the only reason which I would attempt to assign for the cruel defiance of concord is this,—that as the Devil has, since the time of Tartini, possessed the reputation of a good ear for music, and as bells are said to scare evil spirits, so the ingenious Flemings think to accelerate his departure by leaving theirs in so cruel a state of disagreement. If I am mistaken in this conjecture, let it pass: but I would put it to the consciences of the burgomasters of Antwerp, whether innocent travellers who arrive in their city, with a delicate organization of the ear, should be tormented four times an hour, or have their nerves irritated by the constant repetition of the same tune, especially when they are not used to impress upon one any moral duty, as the chimes in some of the London churches do, in one of which I remember to have heard, as a funeral procession entered the churchyard, the tune " Life let us cherish" with real edification.

The external glory of the cathedral is much injured by its being hemmed in by houses; but in viewing the internal structure, I felt the truth of Gibbon's observation, " all superfluous ornament is

rejected by the cold frugality of the Protestants;
but the Catholic superstition, which is always the
enemy of reason, is often the parent of the arts."
The object of the builders seems to have been just
the reverse of that which at the present day raises
us a church with as much saved out of it as possible:
—their ambition was to show that they possessed a
wealth of taste able to clothe bare walls with the
richest specimens of human ingenuity, as if they
had only sought a place where to disburthen themselves of their magnificent thoughts—their hidden
corners and obscure nooks show as much elaboration
and finish in some gem which " blushes unseen," as
that part which meets the eye in open day.   Here
are the most charming proportions of length and
height, an " embowed roof," graceful arches, a light
—not of the dim, religious kind, which in the old
aisles of our cathedrals reveals the cold stony memorials of illustrious dead, but a warm mid-day
glare, disclosing Rubens's divine paintings—a
temple of art, where female forms, full of softness
and vitality, the tender Madonna and Child, calm
saints and patient martyrs, rather lead to an enthusiasm for beauty than contemplations on death.   It
is possible to visit this place without being reminded
of one's frail mortality.   Not so in the minsters of

England, which from the frequency of sepulture are half charnel-houses, with some stage of decomposition going forward under our feet at every step we take, and with that hard unyielding marble (so different to the geniality of painting, but the only material that would exist in the damp and black vapours which collect in those buildings), we are filled with melancholy thoughts on the stern necessity which is rigidly imposed alike on poets and heroes, fools and knaves. The genius of our cathedral service and that of the Catholics is essentially different: in the one, all is holy, abstracted, sublime, where the idea of sex and worldly affections cannot interfere with that chilling flesh-creeping solemnity, which "brings all heaven before the eyes;" in the other, human passions, love and tenderness, are ever awakened, and the eye and ear both administer to voluptuous sensations. In this religion the imagination and the senses go hand in hand, and music and perfumes, the luxury of an eastern sultan, induce yearnings not always of the most godly kind; and it is not surprising that that mode of worship should find many followers, where kissing is a duty enjoined in the rubrick, and in which art the priest never fails to give a specimen of his proficiency when *in pontificalibus* he makes the august sacrifice of the mass.—The first musical performance at which I was present was an afternoon service, or complin, as it is called, the work of a native composer of this city named Kraft ; it was accompanied by the organ and a small band of instruments ; but the voices were not sufficiently numerous to convey the sublime emotions which choral music always does when the *tutti* parts are supported by a large and good choir. The violin accompaniments, which were tolerably free, were played with great smoothness, and excellently in tune. The models of this composer seem to be Hasse and Graun, and his composition partook largely of the bad and commonplace old Italian style of melody, containing long-winded solos, passages now obsolete, and sing-song ungraceful ornaments, as far removed from the present notion of musical beauty as the Hottentot Venus from that of Titian. In the fugued points of his choruses the author was more successful, and showed by the flow and smoothness with which they were introduced, that in ecclesiastical harmony and florid counterpoint he was not out of his element, and here his sequences sometimes reminded me of the solid and stately march of Graun.—The organ of the cathedral is good in parts, particularly in the diapasons and soft stops, with pedal pipes which go down to an abyss "not loud but deep:" the chorus is, however, too squalling and not well voiced. The bass of this instrument is evidently of the same family with our own organs of St. Paul's, Westminster Abbey, and some others; where the richness and body of tone speak for the honesty and ability of the builder, and remind us of those good old times when that accursed *trading* nuisance, a contract, was not thought of. One's admiration is extorted at the tasteful design and elaborate workmanship which is manifest on the cases of the organs in Antwerp, and that at the cathedral is built up with a poetical conception of the splendour which befits those enchanted palaces of sound—the " loud uplifted angel-trumpets," at the mouths of the winged musicians that proudly stand on the eminences on each side of the instrument, really give a fresh dignity to its tones in the imagination. To my mind, these graceful figures, which look just about to fly, are never seen to greater advantage than when the organ is pealing forth, with a solemn stepping bass to some procession below ; and I like the idea of putting such a screen over these mechanical contrivances and metal pipes, and of feasting the sight with a pleasure precisely analagous to that which the hearing receives.

At the Dominicans' church the organ-case is still

more wonderful, but the artist has suffered his fancy
to run riot: the carved figures there are a hell-
brood, all monstrous Gorgons and Hydras, such as
might float through the brain in an ugly dream,
" worse than fables yet have feigned, or fear conceived."—I cannot say that the organ-playing of the
Flemish demands much praise; but in stepping into
a Catholic chapel one morning, I was amazed at
hearing the chaunt accompanied with a number of
ascending and descending scales (some of them
chromatic,) played with great velocity by the performer's right hand, while his left hand and feet
sustained the chords. To me this man appeared to
be endeavouring to burlesque religion, and to turn
the service into a joke. But I believe it is unnecessary to cross the water to find that devotional solemnity in music is not considered incompatible with
the nimblest and most volatile finger in the accompanyist. Such impertinence shows that music,
though in the main an intelligible language, is still
variously construed according to the temperament.

Every traveller who is fresh and long-winded,
makes a point of ascending the highest towers of
churches, that he may note the disposition of the
buildings in a city; but I have seldom found that
the love of this kind of survey has outlived more than

two or three experiments ; and a gentleman whom I requested to be my companion in a visit to the tower of Antwerp cathedral, pleaded corpulence as an excuse, with the same earnestness that I have known women at the Old Bailey turn that accidental circumstance to account. As my journey was productive of an involuntary *solo* from the female attendant, and as it may serve as a warning to youth who may incautiously trust themselves on corkscrew staircases with nervous guides, I insert some circumstances of it. Before we had ascended three hundred feet, I began to envy the indefatigable, wizened, and sinewy calves of my conductress, who stumped on in the most unfeeling manner, leaving me, a " puff'd and reckless libertine," to tread that " primrose path of dalliance" as I was best able; but at a part of the ascent in which we were groping our way in utter darkness, my companion discovered amazing sensibility, and began to shriek like one possessed, vociferating a jargon of Flemish, in which, sounds like Ach ! Ach ! meun Gott ! meun Gott ! were easily distinguishable. The woman was soon completely overcome with fright and exertion, and stood gasping for breath, and a hoarse deprecating voice, which now mingled in with her little ejaculations, did not tend to diminish my surprise ; but after a due administration of snuff and apologies, my guide became calm, and the crowd of horrible imaginings which had rushed into my mind at first, now vanished, and gave place to fancies of a more agreeable kind. The cause of the sudden ebullition was this : a sailor lay up the stairs on his back fast asleep, his legs as usual apart; the woman had entered the cavity, and had also walked a considerable distance on his stomach before she was aware of the peculiar nature of the soil; and her outcries were raised, as she afterwards told me, not from remorse at travelling over his epigastric region without a passport, but from the horror that she was trespassing on the carcass of a huge dog, with whose notions of retributive justice she soon expected to be made acquainted.   Since this adventure, my desires have been less aspiring, a first-floor window contents me, and I have abjured the society of those who live by the disbursement of the oil of their knee joints, and no longer countenance by example an extravagant expenditure of that secretion.

On the festival of Corpus Christi, a mass by Righini was substituted at the cathedral for one of Haydn, which had been promised; and on this occasion the wind instruments were supplied by the military band resident in the city, and the chorus was augmented. The regular installment of a regimental band in the service of the church here, has raised the suggestion why in these " piping times of peace," when men have no longer to play the double bassoon on a forced march, the assistance of those people might not be required for charitable musical performances at home; if such regulations were consistent with military discipline, it would make music cheaper, and in part remove the objections which have been raised to the uselessness of a standing army. Righini is chiefly known to the English amateur through the medium of Mr. Latrobe's valuable collection of sacred music; but detached and isolated specimens give but an imperfect idea of his excellence as a composer, for which purpose it is absolutely necessary to hear an entire work performed. An Italian, bitten with the love of German harmonies, and naturalized and adopted into that school, makes an excellent musician: melody is his paternal inheritance; he has only to acquire a better method of clothing its nakedness than is usual among his countrymen. Cherubini, who has run something into the extreme of learned accompaniment, when in a happy vein, shows that the union of the two schools leaves nothing to be wished in a composer. The Kyrie of Righini's mass in D, which opened in the minor, was particularly impressive from the solemnity of the movement and the independence and boldness of the accompaniments, and had it not been deformed by a frequent recurrence to the major, it might have been taken for Haydn; but there seems a want of consistency in changing the character of the music, while the expression of the words is invariably melancholy and penitential. The " Et Incarnatus est," with clarionet *obligato*, struck me as full of elegance and feeling; but it was much injured in the performance by the bad intonation of the accompanyist, who was, alas! no Willman, and played much too sharp. In Antwerp the wind-instrument players are raw and imperfect, and deficient either in ear or in the management of their instruments. The orchestra, which contains the performers on a flat surface, without that gradual inclination to which we are accustomed, would be unfavourable to experienced artists, and is much more so to these ignorant soldiers. The trumpets were played with so strange a tone, that it was difficult to recognize them in their curious disguise. Though many of the passages of melody in this composition are no longer consistent with the modern taste, I may safely assert, that in a well-worked fugue, and an artfully constructed chorus, few composers excel Vincenzo Righini. On the conclusion of this service, which was to me a perfect curiosity, the organist played a *sortie* of that frivolous, inconsistent character, which seems to be peculiarly admired in Brabant; and which was neither more nor less than one of Nicolai's old harpsichord sonatas, lifted out of its quiet obscurity to the music-desk of a cathedral, a place where its author, in the highest intoxication of vanity, could hardly have fancied it. Though harpsichord music, or pianoforte music, or even harp music, may be accommodated to the organ, provided it contains sequences, or something grave in its construction, it appears a strange perversity of choice to fix upon a piece which is diametrically opposed to these qualifications. The organist, after the service, justified his selection by observing, that a gay style best suited the frame of mind in which the priests and congregation found themselves after discharging their spiritual duties, and that a brisk movement had great effect in creating an appetite for dinner. Whether the gentleman's argument were founded in fact or not, I have ever found the Catholics after mass, and on festivals especially, more tenacious of their dishes and wine, more joyous and convivial than on other days. The whole of Antwerp may be con-

sidered as one vast monument of the genius of Reubens, whose name is almost as much identified with
architecture and sculpture, as his hand is acknow-
ledged by the judge of painting. The idolatry
with which this master is mentioned would, if real,
be such as befits the immortal benefactor of the city;
but there is a great deal of *mock* enthusiasm, which
results from, and is the reflection of the admiration
of strangers, who are constantly visiting his shrine.
It is a misfortune that every idle vagabond who has
learned to name Reubens, thinks himself entitled to
pester a visitor with his tedious and mercenary explanations; and if his services are not accepted, con-
tinues to stick as **perseveringly as** the Old Man of
the Sea stuck to Sinbad, not actually mounted on
one's back, but still not to be shaken off without
some roughness. A guide, who held an official
situation in the church of St. James, where the monument of Reubens is to be seen, called my attention to the portrait of his mistress as the Virgin ;
which, with those of his father, his wives, and himself in a rich suit of armour, standing in a knightly
and commanding attitude, form a handsome altar-
piece : it is a strange allegorical composition, in
which all the prominent characters are sacred ; and
the man said, with much simplicity, that the painter

was obliged to represent them in that way, for as mere portraits they could not have occupied the situation in the church they do. The extraordinary capability manifested by this good Catholic of viewing the picture at once in its religious and profane aspect, amused me, and it is, I think, as curious an instance of *make-believe* and wilful self-deception as human nature can furnish. It was a bold scheme of the artist to turn his favourite into a real goddess; she sits there (unconscious of more vows and prayers than were offered to her in life-time) in an eternal silence, scarcely interrupted by the tender and graceful strains of the " Benedictus."—In contemplating the celestial faces with which the walls are adorned, one must remark the strong sympathy which exists between their expression, and that of parts of the musical service; and though music has, according to Milton, been long " married to immortal Verse," in Antwerp she more than flirts with Painting.—The church of the Dominican friars is worth examination, though deformed with the most base and contemptible monuments of monkish superstition; such, for instance, as their famed rareeshow, called Calvary, where, through a small iron grating, is to be seen the image of Christ, dressed in his grave habiliments, and inhabiting the se-

pulchre, neighboured by a large company of both
sexes in hell, with good red-hot flames lapping about
them, and who seem to enjoy that novel kind of
warm bath with the most lively consciousness.   At
this representation my guide was so diabolically har-
dened as to grin instead of invoking St. Anthony to
save him from that fiery gulf to which, for aught I
knew, he possessed as good a claim as any of the
harmless salamanders who were inhabiting it.——An
artist, whose name was I believe Breughel, has
enriched the Dominicans' church, as well as the
cathedral, with unrivalled specimens of art in carved
wood ; he has supported every confessional box with
two standing figures, with such an endless variety
in the disposal of them, that each demands a separate and attentive scrutiny.   The drapery of many
of these is executed with wonderful freedom, and
the faces have a great distinctness of character ; it
is easy here to choose whether to unpack a cargo
of peccadilloes behind the back of the bald-headed,
long-bearded prophet, who holds a stern, heaven
ward look, or to creep behind the rueful and com
passionate Magdalen.   But the most remarkable
instance of finished workmanship in carving, is the
pulpit of the cathedral, which is surrounded with
the quaintest and oddest congregation of birds in

grotesque but natural attitudes, and is an eminence from which the dullest homily might be endured with patience. The grim, down-looking wolves' heads which our forefathers have made pendent from the sides of their churches, the fantastic laughter-moving visage which one sometimes discovers on an old dark pannel in a choir, seem just as appropriate appendages of those places as the denizens of the farm-yard are to the pulpit ; and I can hardly envy the sensations of the preacher who ascends one by a sort of Jacob's ladder, amidst turkey-cocks, geese, hens, and other fowl. If any disposition to sacrilege is felt in looking over the churches, it is certainly when one finds in a little box with a glass door, an image of the Virgin dressed after the fashion of a large doll, and beplastered with ornaments that look like the pewter dishes little children play with ; the vulgar finery destroys the sentiment ; the mother caressing her baby is prettier to my mind than the rampant queen of heaven. For the rude crucifix placed upon the naked sea-beach by poor adventurous fishermen, the object to which their thoughts turn on many a dark and blowing night, I profess a reverence.

There is no public secular music of any kind to be heard in this city, with the exception of the vile scraping which is endured at the dinner-table of the inn, an infliction which irritates the nerves, and stops the concoctive process. Music is too heavenly an art to be degraded into mere sauce, without a protest, though that be useless; if it be good, it cannot be co-enjoyed with mouthfuls of ragout; if bad, it gives me indigestion. Music engrosses, it " kills the flock of all affections else that live in us," and though it rather encourages wine-drinking and luxurious excitement, it resents that one should satisfy the grosser animal wants and the etherial nature at the same time. Hogarth has, in his Enraged Musician, given the portraiture of my friend Dr. H——; when any sudden and impertinent eruption of sound distracts his attention from what Serjeant Dalgetty terms the onslaught, he cordially hates this dinner harmony, and consigns it with the sorrel soup of France and the white soup of Germany, to everlasting perdition.

I had the pleasure of spending a musical evening with M. Le Brun, a resident of Antwerp, and the early friend of Haydn; a gentleman who, in a green and lusty old age, shows a pleasing bigotry and exclusiveness of preference for the works of his old companion. As that war of words in which I have been frequently engaged for the respective supre-

macy of Handel, Haydn, Sebastian Bach, and
Mozart, has become a tiresome service, partly out
of civility as a guest, and partly out of a consciousness of having been a renegade at different times
from one cause to the other, I on this occasion
quietly allowed Haydn to receive the palm. The
niece of M. Le Brun, who has been a pupil of
Woelfl, showed an admirable discretion in the performance of some of Haydn's pianoforte sonatas,
particularly in that set dedicated to Madame Bar-
tolozzi, as well as in a sonata in four flats, written by
the author for Hummel when a boy, and she discovered a firmness of hand, and cultivated taste in
adagio playing, which I have never yet heard
equalled by a female performer. After hearing
these masterly compositions, I could not but regret
the innovations that have crept in upon the style of
writing for the instrument; the search after effects
of light and shade, instead of a succession of good
musical ideas; crude harmonies, and violent changes,
instead of a flow of natural modulation. Although
this lady is in the constant receipt of the newest
capricios and fantasias which are produced by the
lightning-fingered virtuosi resident in Paris, they
remain untouched in her portfolio from her inability
to discover their meaning; but the charm of

Haydn's pianoforte music remains ever fresh and undecayed.

The last musical service which took place during my stay in Antwerp, was performed in the cathedral at night; it was delightful to stand at the extremity of the nave, and, through the long vista of arches, enveloped in thick darkness, to see the blaze of torch-light thrown on the high altar, the gorgeous robes of the priests, the swinging of silver censers which warm the air and embalm the pictures in their fragrance and aroma; above all, to hear Gregorian phrases softened and mellowed by distance, the effect of the whole was so overpowering as easily to make one credit those tales of overwrought fancy, where people have suddenly imagined themselves sublimed, deified, ecstatic. The reason is at first taken prisoner, and there is little inclination to question the import of rites and ceremonies, to which all the noblest arts are made subservient and tributary; but the mind at last works out its own salvation, seizes what is good and admirable, and soon, in one of these edifices, as in a Pagan temple, worships the spirit of Beauty in all its forms, forgetful that uncharitableness and bigotry exist in the world. It is a pity that women's voices are not enlisted in the service of the mass at Antwerp; these kind of

soprani are much better adapted than boys for the
sort of expression which modern Catholic music
requires, especially in the refined solos of Mozart
and Haydn; the charm of pathos and simplicity
which belong to the latter class of performers is here
thrown away; and though the passages may be correct as to the text, they ill assort with the childish
pipers that give them utterance. When the young
singers have passed over that part of their lives so
prettily described by Cherubino in Mozart's Figaro,
" Non so piu," if they have previously given promise, nature no longer withholds from them that last
best gift, the indefinable charm which distinguishes
the style of genius from that of line-and-rule correctness, be it called soul, sensibility, or what it
may. I have never heard playing or singing from
children, however far they might be advanced in
the mechanical part of the science, which possessed
this quality.

Every composer who writes music for the Catholic service makes the Virgin an ideal mistress; as
Solomon addressed the church in his Canticles,
calling her " soft names in many a mused rhyme,"
so does the musician exhaust his fancy in tender
phrases for the " Mater divinæ gratiæ," and the
" Mater amabilis:" the best and most impassioned

songs of the ancient opera school are poured forth by the singer, who addresses under these words some less exalted but more substantial divinity. A little of this leaven will mingle in the service of religion, where the spiritual and carnal boundaries of musical expression are not better defined. In England it is difficult for a music lover to pass a cathedral in which the organ is sounding, without stepping in for the sake of the plagal cadence, a piece of simple grandeur, which will always, while our nature remains, affect powerfully : but in Antwerp there is not only this attraction, but also the most inventive and florid compositions; and though the performance is a little rough, and the attention much interrupted by the scuffling on the pavement of the cathedral, yet the matter is frequent, and is accomplished out of pure love, and not as a job to be despatched.

The music here costs nothing, and it is heartily to be wished that not only the cheapness, but the modesty of the performance, were paralleled with us. The cantor informed me, that though their library contains the works of the great masters of Germany and Italy, they do not wish to hack their Haydn and Mozart by too frequent repetition, but reserve them for holidays and extraordinary feasts.

During mass, a tall gaunt Swiss, armed with an

enormous halberd, stalks up and down the cathedral, the terror of those who turn their backs upon
the host; and it is surprising, that among so much
to soften and ameliorate the asperities of the tem-
per, this fellow should be ever brooding mischief,
never appearing so happy as when dealing his
" apostolic blows" among the little boys, who occasionally collect in a crowd round some one of the
doors. The sight of an unsheathed blade in a
Christian temple is an eye-sore; and the hired ruf-
fian who carries it was to me so personally obnoxious,
that when I found it necessary to ask some questions, and to pay him for his trouble in answering,
the fierceness of my manner made me laugh in-
wardly.—Though the Flemings are jealous of the
respect due to the offices of their religion, and prepare to thrust offenders against it in the abdomen
(at what point of enormity this takes place I have
not yet learned), they take a strange licence themselves. At a book-shop under the very nose of the
church, and surrounded by missals, devout exercises, sacrifices to holy hearts, &c. I found a Bac-
chanalian sermon, burlesquing outright the Scriptural
quotations used in preaching, and substituting Bac-
chus, Cupid, and Apollo, for the names of the
Trinity, with a text worthy of that "master of

scoffing," Rabelais.—" Den Hemel drinkt, den Aerde drinkt, waerom zouden wy niet drinken ?"— " The heavens drink, the earth drinks, why should not we drink ?"—an appeal quite irresistible, enforced by good wine.

I do not think the people in Flanders are hypocrites, and secretly contemn the religion they profess ; but they are so intimate with the whole heavenly host, so much hand-in-glove with the saints, whose faces and figures they recognize as duly as one merchant does another on change, that it is no wonder if their reverence for them gets a little rusty.

The great pictures of Rubens which adorn each side of the passage to the high altar, arrest the steps of every passenger in the cathedral, whether native or foreign ; and it must fulfil the highest ambition of a painter to have his works placed in a magnificent building, where they are never without eyes upon them. The Descent from, and Elevation of, the Cross, appeared never to be deserted, but to be giving pleasure to fresh spectators the whole day. A poem or an oratorio cannot be enjoyed by snatches, but one may spend ten minutes over a great picture with real improvement : the eye takes in so much more at once than the ear. —What a triumph for the artist is it that these great works look now as fresh as if they had just left the easel! The most inveterate caviller must, I think, own the Descent from the Cross a faultless production, whether propriety of the composition, expression, or colouring, is concerned. There is a divine aspect of goodness in the face of each figure, which renders some atonement to the feelings for the sight of the horrible and cruel death which has been suffered. The wings of these pictures are, with the true prodigality of genius, made as attractive as the principal: the figure of the Virgin in the Annunciation, who is *enceinte*, and stepping to the house of Zacharias, has really borrowed tenfold grace from that circumstance. In the Purification, on the other wing, the grand wrinkled face and thick beard of the old Simeon, who, in his pompous vestments, is holding a sprawling naked infant; the restrained eagerness of the mother, who with extended hands waits to receive her first-born, are profound in the conception and execution. In another place the artist has introduced a child, who is disturbed at the breast, and lays his cheek against it: the action is not more natural than the rosy tinge and the pulpy softness of its flesh. Rubens gives the naked figure as faithfully after nature as any one: others may make it look handsomer, but he gives the real thing.   If he paints a woman's bosom, he paints it like one who is intimately acquainted with the subject.   In the unconscious look of children, and in the full-blown mature beauty of his golden-haired women, Rubens is admirable.

COLOGNE.

AMONG the violin-players of England, and the various amateurs of instrumental quartetts and sinfonias, there have been some hardy enough to assert that church music is always the same; and of the former, a leader of the Philharmonic Concert is reported to have said, that "if the whole of Handel's works were at the bottom of the sea, it would not give him the slightest regret." Without expecting any very just or enthusiastic remark on the science from a *mere* player, and especially on the violin, nothing can be more silly than the supposition that the vagaries of the quartett style are the only real creations in music. Though the delicacy of a well-written quartett, or the fancy, and light and shade of a sinfonia, fill the hearer with delight, it is reserved for choral sacred compositions to awaken that profound emotion which attends a perception of the sublime.

One of those processions of the town inhabitants, frequent in Catholic countries, took place in Cologne on Sunday morning, during the octave from

the great feast Corpus Domini, and the music which
accompanied it placed the combinations and effects
of the art in an entirely new position.   On these
occasions the streets are strewed with rushes, so that
the performers glide along noiseless as ghosts, and
nothing interrupts the solemnity of the harmony.
The singers consisted of young girls and boys,
youths and maidens, and lastly of consummate men,
walking in double rows of immense length, and
sometimes accompanied by bands of wind instruments.   The simple hymn, sung by the girls in
three parts, pitched in a low key, nicely in tune,
and without any vociferation—this, replied to by
the men's voices, and then in return by those of the
youths, produced the most affecting appeal to the
feelings of which music is capable—tears came un-
bidden.   The pauses in the music, the large body
of voices, the contrast between the trebles, tenors,
and basses, the sudden breaking out in different
parts of that long line, some voices from their distance merging into silence, others unexpectedly
swelling out near at hand, produced an entire and
delicious novelty in the art, and such as might by a
great master of effect be turned to infinite account.
—It would be gratifying to try how a regular motett
for several choirs, of slow movement and artful

counterpoint, with judicious marks of piano and forte, would succeed, the performers being placed in bodies at certain distances apart. I am sanguine in the conviction, that an extensive and entirely untrodden field of exertion is open to a composer; but in this, as well as in orchestral writing, great experience and actual experiment are necessary to success. In the present instance, the ear was not offended by any jarring or discordant harmony, because the signals for the different parties to begin were regulated with judgment, one not commencing until the other had stopped. The priests, however, who took upon themselves to roar the Gregorian chaunt, made great blunders in the harmony; their basses and appoggiature were uniformly wrong. Two horns, clarionets, bassoons, and a bass trombone, played in a smooth manner and extremely subdued, supplied the place of an itinerant organ, and supported the voices in those parts where the modulation was somewhat more learned than suits merely vocal music.

The cathedral, or *Dom Kirche*, as it is called, is remarkable for three things—its architecture, its large bell, and its organ. Though a great part of this magnificent pile remains unfinished, some of the roof being merely boarded, there is no building

which one enters with more hushed and awe-stricken
sensations. It has not the cheerful gravity of Antwerp, nor indeed of Catholic edifices in general;
but has more of the gloom of our own minsters, is
of enormous length, and the choir is an unrivalled
specimen of lightness and elegance. I was never
so much delighted with the richness of a single
sound as when the great bell of this cathedral was
ringing, and heard on the marble pavement of the
church ; the tone, which was continuous, resembled
a gigantic bass diapason pipe. For mere tone this
was the purest, weightiest, and finest I ever heard,
the most poetical piece of monotony in the world.
There can be no musician in Cologne who does not
sympathise with this vast machine when those
mighty throbs are running through its quivering,
sensitive body; when it speaks it begets instant attention. The two rivals of this bell are at Erfurt
and Vienna, but I prefer the tone of the one here.

Although high mass did not take place in the
cathedral as usual, I had the good fortune, in attending vespers, to hear the magnificent organ,
which is one of the largest and most glorious instruments in the world : the compass is about the
same as that at St. Paul's ; in body and weight of
tone it is still richer, and is more equal throughout

in the bass notes; their fine roll and " sweet thunder " will ever remain in my memory. Sebastian
Bach, with his resonant fugues, might here have
reigned and revelled, but such was not the will of
fate. The organist was extremely bad, and if one
may deduce such a conclusion from his playing, a
flippant coxcomb; his interludes between the Gregorian tones amazed me, from their unreligious and
anomalous mixture of the music of a ballet or tea-
garden with the cloistral severity of the chaunt.
To show how little the correspondence of time or
character is regarded in some parts of the Continent
I have noted one or two bars as a curiosity.

This kind of waltz movement was, by some curious alchymy of mind, thought to be a becoming
handmaiden to the fifth tone.

Who can refrain, in witnessing so wanton and
gratuitous an exhibition of folly, from wishing for
some such interruption to the performer as Sir Toby
longs for, when Malvolio is soliloquizing " Oh for
a stone bow to hit him in the eye !" but where, as

here, for religion may be understood blind bigotry
and fanaticism, an obtuseness to real violations of
good taste, and a more bold profanity may be observed. The priests take snuff, joke, and grin
together while they are before the altar, or sitting
in the choir; in the streets they look starched,
prim, and sanctified. The Gregorian service was
performed in a manner the most remote from good
musicianship, every verse being accompanied with
the same harmonies, so that there was nothing more
than a tiresome repetition of tonic and dominant:
as Handel was wont to remark when present at bad
music, " Now A is trumps, now D." The churches
are free from that intolerable nuisance in those of
France, the serpent, the sound of which so much
resembles the immature efforts and bleating of a
bull-calf; neither is the eye disgusted with the
poverty-stricken appearance of the usual rush-bot-
tomed chairs and bare deal forms which break the
grandeur of a building into petty detail and poor
convenience. During my stay in Cologne there
were no operas performed, a circumstance the less
regretted, as the uncouth manners and staring ill-
breeding of the Walloons did not promise much for
musical taste. At an hotel I was however much
pleased with a trio for the harp, violin, and viola;

a very good composition in C minor, and in the *agitato* style, which was played with great neatness and expression. A young girl who played the harp possessed abilities which would have procured her in England an income of hundreds a year, and applause at the first-rate concerts ; and yet with this talent, and the manners and dress of a lady, she depends on the contributions of a casual audience for her reward. The modest self-appreciation of this young person, and the respect with which her hearers treated her, were equally complimentary to both parties.

Those in England who have studied the German language in the dialect of Gottingen or Dresden, and (as usually happens) make their first essay in speaking at one of the towns on the Rhine, must not be disheartened at not being able to understand or to make themselves understood by the inhabitants. Many Germans have assured me that the patois of Cologne is unintelligible even to them, as it approximates more to the Dutch than to their own language. In a dilemma with respect to the coin, I was referred for explanation to a man living in the hotel, who called himself an Irishman, who, so far from using the brogue of the Emerald Isle, was unable to speak more than three words of English, and those were all devoted to affirmations on the subject of his place of nativity. It does a little constrain politeness to acknowledge as a countryman one who runs out the whole stock of his mother-tongue with such extreme rapidity.

The *eil wagen* * which runs between Cologne and Frankfort is a commodious vehicle, and if the scent of tobacco be not objected to, an agreeable one. A kind of blue smock-frock, which is here worn by all sorts of travellers, sets aside every distinction of rank, and leaves the owner to recommend himself merely by urbanity of manners and politeness. These machines are rarely devoid of material for observation. One of my companions on this journey was a fat Amsterdam merchant, who had visited the baths of Aix la Chapelle on account of a disordered stomach, and who sat in one corner of the coach, discoursing of sauces and wines, and of what was *lecker* (delicious), though at the very time he could hardly open his eyes from intense head-ache. There is something amounting to the *heroic* in this mode of paying the penalty of sensual indulgence without puling or complaint; the virtues of attachment and endurance relieve the grossness of the character, and

* Post coach.

we half respect the magnanimous glutton, who
" eats and writhes, and eats and writhes again."

In passing through Bonn it was my intention to
have visited the amiable and excellent musician
Ferdinand Ries, to whom I was furnished with let-
ters ; but having previously learned that he was on
a journey to the interior, this pleasure was prevented. The retirement of Bonn must be doubly
endeared to one who has known what the task is to
listen to the blunders of school-girls, with the
mania of composition upon him. Teaching under
such circumstances is the most melancholy and
galling sacrifice that a musician can make of himself.

FRANKFORT.

DOES any one wish to attain the summit of earthly
bliss? If so, let him travel in fine summer
weather between Mayence and Frankfort, take his
dinner in a pleasant chamber, overlooking that
smiling country, with the welcome intrusion of
green boughs at the window, and after emptying a
flask of old Hockheimer, he will arrive at the
blessed consummation. The merit of this discovery
I must share with a certain German student, and
we both flatter ourselves to have appreciated that
ecstatic state described in the old ballad :

> " For what more can a man desire,
> Nor sitting by a sea-coal fire," &c.

Rhenish must surely have been the wine to which
Milton alluded when he talked of *rising* afterwards
" to hear the lute well touched:" it is the most
poetical and inspiring of fluids ; it gives excitement
without muzziness, cheerfulness without conglome-
ration. Port wine has spoiled much music, has led
to much inefficient fingering, and many wrong

chords. The time is now fortunately past when it was usual for gentlemen to repair after dinner to the company of the ladies in the drawing-room, with shining faces, eyes *set* in their heads, lazy tongues to applaud in the style of Cassio, " 'Fore heav'n, that is more exquisite song than the other;" but even in mere criticism (easier than playing) our strong wines induce no wonderful acumen.

Although the tour of the Rhine is now almost as well known as the voyage to Margate, it would be a sullenness, an ingratitude, to that land of vineyards, of romance, and sunshine, as well as to our worthy host, not to say how much we enjoyed a sojourn at a long, low, white house near Mayence, situate on the very brink of the Rhine, where the monks were formerly supreme, and where their skill in cookery is still emulated. The waiters at this inn are full of legendary lore, and relate the history of Sir Roland with so much enthusiasm, that they appear to have descended from a race of chroniclers; and the country is so romantic, that one would be transported back to the age of chivalry, except for that vile modern necessity of settling one's bill.

It was in the cheerful city of Frankfort that I first became acquainted with German operatic performances. The opera-house here may, at a rough guess, be compared in size to the Lyceum Theatre; and it does not appear very favourable to the conveyance of sound, if one may so judge from the flatness with which it falls upon the ear. The orchestra consists of about forty-five musicians, of which the wind instruments, particularly the horns and clarionets, are good, but the stringed band wants weight as well as more bass; the violins seem to be always *con sordini*. The performers, both vocal and instrumental, are all under the domination of the opera director; who, placed on an elevation in the front of the orchestra, gives the cue to all, very properly setting aside the offices of leader, chorus director, &c. which in England frequently causes the band and singers to be wandering in opposite directions. M. Guhr, who is maestro di capella, and director of the music at the Frankfort Theatre, takes his stand with the score before him and his baton of office, and sees that the musicians attend to their parts, though there seems to be little fear that they will be omitted through carelessness and indifference. The musicians in London, particularly the wind-instrument players, often exasperate a composer by omitting the *solos* which are set down for them, and from the lenience of the leader towards these mistakes, the poor author frequently receives the most unjust misrepresentation.

Boieldieu's opera, "Das * weisse Fräulein," was in fashion during my visit to Frankfort, and nothing could exceed the regularity and precision in which the choruses in it were performed; throughout the whole, the *ensemble* was strict, and the nicety of intonation exact; the accompanied recitatives, or rather *musica parlante*, in which the instruments are not regulated by any definite time, reminded me of the best days of our Italian opera. Here is a very agreeable tenor singer, M. Nieser, whose voice in the sweetness of its quality resembles that of Curioni; but with this advantage, that it is always in tune, and that his style is destitute of all flummery and impertinence. I was pleased to hear theatrical music without those vulgar appeals in the shape of long shakes, tremendous roars, runs and cadences of all kinds, the abomination of our public performances; and though they produce applause, so easily acquired that few of our singers cannot boast a good stock of them. M. Dobler, a bass singer, must be also recorded as possessing a pretty good voice—perhaps

* In Germany it would appear that white and ghostly young ladies are of the neuter gender.

a little too fat and *quaggy* in its depth if rigorously
criticised. The theatre is not rich in female
talent; yet the performance of Mademoiselle Haus
deserves notice, not only from the unpretending
style in which she executed her songs, but from
the very remarkable facility with which she reached
and dwelt upon the highest notes. Mademoiselle

Haus sang up to with perfect ease, and that
not as a matter of display, but in following the
author's text. A *bravura* song in F, satisfied me
of this extraordinary gift. The concerted pieces,
which best show the strength of an opera company,
were very long; and here, as the quality of the
voices did not provoke individual criticism, I was
much pleased by the musician-like style in which
they were performed. No ornamental notes were
introduced which did not belong to the harmony,
a sin of which public singers are too frequently
guilty, and which results from the want of a well-
grounded education in the science. How often,
for instance, has Mozart's little duett, "Su l'Aria,"
been sung in London by two fashionable singers,
who concluded by making a shake on fourths—

The secret of the extraordinary popularity which Boieldieu's opera receives may be traced to the admiration of Walter Scott's works, which is excessive in Germany : as a composition, it is full of the worst instances of French taste. Noise, violent changes of key, and that species of modulation which may be termed *baroque*, are its characteristics. The well-trained ear is little prepared for such a remorseless succession of harmonies as this :—C, B flat, E flat, B natural, without preparation or management. The auction scene, in the finale to the second act of Boieldieu's opera, which I have heard extolled as a masterpiece on the authority of the late Weber, appears to me to fall ludicrously below the eulogium : the situation seems to promise some opportunity for varieties of character in dramatic composition, but the result does not bear out the supposition.

The theatre here opens at six o'clock, and the whole is over before nine, as afterpieces and farces are wisely omitted for the enjoyment of a lounge in the public gardens.

The unostentatious and impressive nature of the Lutheran Confirmation Service has been already set forth by Madame de Stael; and it is, I think, the only interesting thing in the whole catalogue of

their religious observances. I attended a service
of this sort in the principal Lutheran church,
where the children, alternately with the whole congregation, sang verses of those unsophisticated
finely harmonized tunes which are distinguished
by the name of *corale.* The peculiarity of the
singing in a German congregation is its univer-
sality and general correctness of tune. A multitudinous shout of this kind must affect the most
phlegmatic mortal; and even Whitefield confesses
his emotion at hearing some thirty thousand on a
hill side uplift their voices in a stave. The effect
of the organ is in this church much deteriorated by
its being thrust *close* to the ceiling; whereas had
a good space been left between it and the roof, for
the sounds to play about, the tone would have a
fairer chance. To ascertain the truth of this observation, I need only request a comparison between
the two cases to be made, and would recommend
the consideration of it to those who are concerned
in the erection of instruments in our own churches.

I have scarcely yet met with one organist whose
playing accords with the genius of his instrument,
or who possesses the grave style that becomes it.
The workmen here are not so good as their tools,
and they display a wonderful liking for *twiddling*

with the solo stops, instead of mingling three or four parts in one confluence of harmony.

The concerts in Frankfort are given at the Red House. A sinfonia by Wranisky in F, and one by Haydn in E flat, were extremely well played, and gave me much pleasure; but the number and quality of the pieces introduced at the concerts will not induce a musical amateur to reside long here. The last performance consisted of an overture by Cherubini, a horn solo, a violin solo, and a couple of songs by Paer—neither too long nor too good a selection. The two principal music-shops are amply supplied with the writings of Fürstenau for the flute, and of Czerny for the pianoforte; but manifest a "plentiful lack" of scores.

Although my visits to the Catholic cathedral in the old city have been assiduous (as more than half the towns-people are Lutherans), the aisles of that most ancient structure have remained voiceless. Any lover of antiquity and romance will be well repaid in looking over this place, the sides of which are covered with helmets, gauntlets, trophies, armorial bearings, the petrified figures of knights armed at all points, standing on swans, dogs, or gryphons, and cracked down the middle by age, but whose stiff rigid figures and hard faces show them equally formed to give and receive knocks; and it is neither matter of surprise nor of regret that some of these gentry, after passing through the vicissitudes of this mortal life, should have received their *coup de grace* so early as the year 756, and have ever since left their stone effigies silently looking out from those walls. Old Froissart has, doubtless, commemorated their achievements, and chaunted over them his usual requiem, " God assoyle their souls."

DARMSTADT.

In this part of the world travelling is the only expensive article. The Prince of Tour and Taxis is the general postmaster; and his title is well deserved, for he indeed taxes tourists. The grandduke, here resident, is the most renowned amateur of Germany, and personally encourages the art and its professors.

The pleasantest compensation for a hot and dusty ride, is to find, on arriving at a fresh town, an opera going forward: this was my happy case at Darmstadt, for the rehearsal of Weber's Euryanthe was to take place in the evening. The only requisite to obtain admission was to send in a card; and though I arrived before business had commenced, and while the house was but dimly lighted, to find my knees knocking against the benches of the pit was so well-known a sensation as to translate me into an instant familiarity with the place. It is to many in London no unamusing pastime to sit shrouded in darkness, and to witness the wordy contests of the maestro, the prima donna,

and the leader, &c.; all the foaming disputes, the
stamping, shrieking, and raving, that must *of necessity* precede the production of an Italian opera.
What can equal the rage of an incensed operatic
heroine, whom beauty and the consciousness of
talent have both combined to make wilful !—it
must have blows.   Many a time has the poor
conductor (thy skull, unfortunate Scappa ! is now
in my mind's eye) had his head hammered with a
thick score, for not being sufficiently prompt in his
obedience to the word of command.   At Darmstadt
all is quietly and peaceably managed, probably
because the grand-duke himself superintends the
rehearsals.   This venerable nobleman, now between
seventy and eighty years of age, may on such occasions be generally seen standing at a music-desk
on the stage, and directing the orchestra with the
blandest and most affable demeanour.   He appears
to be the remnant of a tall well-built man, though
his military uniform and sword show as if in mockery
of a paralytic contraction which has bowed the
wearer's head nearly to his chest.   The grand-duke
is, however, still capable of considerable vivacity,
which I am informed he principally displays in
saluting those ladies who sing to his satisfaction ;
he is lucky if in the discharge of this important

duty he meets with few struggles, much less an imitation of the classic flight of Arethusa from Alpheus.

The road to promotion and court favour in this little state lies in musical skill, for an aide-de-camp of the duke's gave the time to the choruses; so that with this exalted assistance the capell-meister, M. Mongald, had nearly a sinecure.—The rehearsal was soon despatched, as the opera had been before played, and the duke merely required a *finale* and one or two other movements to be tried.

Darmstadt is a place of splendid buildings, squares, and fountains; there is no poverty to be seen about it; and so great is the courtesy of the inhabitants to a stranger, that it becomes almost a necessity that he walk with his hat in his hand. Their politeness is entirely free from servility, it springs from kindness of heart; and where, in a thinly-peopled state, one has leisure for these urbanities, they are worth all the less exacting but stupid and brutal sulkiness to be found in the world.

About ten steps from the door of the opera-house lead to the open gardens of the duke, and thus may be enjoyed at the same time the highest luxury of a civilized city and rural life. It is in

this quiet retirement, and in the calmness of evening, that the beauty of music and the merits of
performers are generally discussed ; and among the
youths and maidens there appear sundry other dis-
cussions, to which green trees, moonlight, a soft air,
and the fragrance of flowers are marvellous incen-
tives. I could not help envying the peaceful life of
some of the musicians, whom I met after their
pleasant labour returning home alone by these
beautiful paths. There can be no fitter place for
the chewing the cud of a pleasant fancy, or for
feeling the "dainty sweet" of "lovely melancholy."

I was induced to visit the palace chapel, in which
the Lutheran service is performed, but was griev-
ously disappointed in the expectation of hearing
some good music. Since I left England my ears
have not suffered such pains and penalties, and on
this occasion I experienced that Germans *may* and
can sing out of tune ; but then their psalm was an
interminable one, and would have tried the ears and
lungs of the very best singers. The subject of the
preacher's oration was the mutability of sublunary
affairs, and his view of it for a divine equally new
and philosophical ; for instead of inculcating contempt of this world's pleasures, he advised a due
regulation of them as the only means of attaining

an equable flow of happiness, and of preventing repinings and regrets. It was, as one of our revered monarchs used to say, when complimenting his chaplain, a very good, *short* sermon ; and the congregation flocked out to help digest their theological repast with some of the prettiest airs in Rossini's Barbiere di Seviglia, played by the military band on parade. When the Sunday is fine, the half hour between the conclusion of church service and the beginning of dinner may be spent very cheerfully at Darmstadt; the air resounds with waltz tunes, the ladies are out (actually) dressed for the opera in the evening, the soldiers stand in columns, while the officers as usual restrain their exuberant chargers, and (to use Sir Philip Sydney's expression) " now careering it, and now caricoling it," cause an awful devastation of heart among the fair spectators. It must however be asserted in justice to the German ladies, that they are not exclusive in devoting their smiles and good nature to those who have careered it and caricoled it ; a frank and polite address is sure to leave the possessor no cause of complaint. The scene of this Sunday exhibition is on the great square opposite the Exercise Haus, an arsenal, or rather *brazen* harem, where the grand-duke keeps his cannon, with as much horror of a stranger's peeping in upon them, as a Turk would show if his favourite women were in jeopardy.

On the performance of Euryanthe, for the payment of about thirteen pence English I took my place in the pit. Think, gentle reader, of enjoying an opera, played and sung by the best artists, for that sum. The interior of the house is roomy, and handsomely decorated; the band is the largest of Germany; the royal box is placed exactly in front of the stage, and the signs from it are most rigorously attended to during the whole performance. No beacon was ever more zealously watched in war-time than this by the capell-meister. As soon as the grand-duke and his suite were seated, the overture commenced, and it was better played than I remember to have heard it even by the Philharmonic Society in London; the part in which the violins *con sordini* are accompanied by iterated notes on the violas, a very critical passage, was admirably executed; and much effect was produced by the basses leading off the little fugued point *pianissimo*, instead of the contrary, as is generally done. When it is stated that this excellent orchestra numbers seven contra bassi for its foundation, with a corresponding proportion of other instruments, some idea may be formed of the force and dignity with which instrumental pieces are executed. The double basses used in Germany are frequently strung with four instead of three strings, thinner than those in use with us, and descending to E below the usual scale ; when mixed with others the depth and richness they produce are very fine. A *pastorale* movement in D, and a bass song in C minor, were some of the best music of the opera ; but the excellent re-christening of this performance by the amateurs of Berlin, renders all additional remark upon it nugatory. By the amateurs of that city it was unanimously dubbed L'Ennuyante, and truly, if the essence of dryness and head-labour in music may deserve the appellation, it is well bestowed. The pretty passage of melody in the overture, when estimated with reference to other parts of the opera, is as " a drop in the desert ;" and it vexes one that a composer capable of thinking in this way, should choose to batten upon the leavings of other people. Most of Weber's wildest fancies (save and except in the demoniacal Freischütz) are as distinct from true invention as the ravings of madness are from the frenzy of sense—and, between a bedlamite and a poet, heaven knows there is latitude for choice. This is not in-

tended as an irreverend allusion to Weber, but
merely as pushing the comparison to its verge; and
it may be modestly opined, that a little of the ra-
tionality and *sweetness* which Mozart did not
undervalue, might not have lowered the vigorous
imagination and profound knowledge of the orchestra which Weber possessed.—Mademoiselle
Madler, who performed the part of Euryanthe, and
is the principal soprano in this *corps*, has a sweet
voice, and would make an excellent chamber-singer;
but in the *forte* parts of every bravura she was almost inaudible, because the band is really too large
for accompanying opera-music, especially songs.
But whoever looked at Mademoiselle Madler
would hardly wish for a higher pleasure than his
eye-sight would afford him; she is a model of German beauty, which is indeed a condensation of female loveliness, including all the sentiment of it.
The lady must be thus imagined: a being somewhat about the height of Shakespear's Rosalind,
with that undulating flow of outline in her figure
which never wearies in contemplating; a face perfect for its symmetrical regularity, and its look of
goodness; hair (almost distracting to mention) of
an auburn colour, and in such profusion that when
allowed to escape from its confinement, it descended

nearly to the feet. This abundance of hair is the dowry which every German woman brings her husband; and I find that in this country they have engrossed the fabled strength of Samson in that particular, which should by lineal descent have been *ours;* but if they are usurpers, they are certainly not tyrants.——M. Vetter, of Leipsic, who was the first tenor in the opera of Euryanthe, gave me great pleasure as a singer, perfect in every requisite for his art, and sustained his difficult part, in fact the most prominent one of the opera, with great skill. After a Sunday spent in this way, the head is not quite so ripe for the pillow as after wading through a few sections of the Whole Duty of Man; but whether it be the consciousness of sin that keeps one awake, I have not as yet determined.

MUNICH.

THE whole territory between Darmstadt and Munich has been not inaptly called the *golden* country, if that term may describe all that is fertile and picturesque. At Stuttgard I tasted the first and only unpleasant wine perhaps to be found in Germany. The produce of the Neckar vineyards, which is there placed on the dinner-table in unstopped decanters, has a strong resemblance in colour, smell, and taste, to the *gargle* which physicians prescribe for a sore throat.

In Bavaria, the livery, or rather uniform of the postillion (which varies in every state) mounts to an extravagance of absurdity; he here indues black breeches, a yellow fringed jacket, a cocked hat and green feather, and looks half priest, half mountebank, characters which in this country at least are not found to be quite so repugnant to one another as they might be imagined. The German postillion is by no means the phlegmatic person he has been represented; his salary is a fixed one, and therefore

if impudence and cunning were natural to him, he
can have no views on the purses of passengers which
prompt their exercise; the fresh air gives him elastic
and unvarying spirits; he is ever carrolling and
gay, cracking his whip and his jokes, till some en-
tanglement of the harness dashes his merriment;
he stops, groans as he hoists his ponderous boot
over the horse's side, and while remedying the accident is melancholy for two minutes, adjuring by
the " heilege sacrament" these calamities of existence; but when once again seated, he straightway
forgets what manner of man he was.

For some miles before the entrance of Munich,
the eye catches the long chain of Tyrol mountains,
which appear in the horizon with their snow-
crowned heads, hardly distinguishable from clouds;
when the sun is shining, the snow on them, which
glitters like burnished silver on a dark blue ground,
has a very lovely effect. Farther on may be seen
the mountains of Salzburg, from behind which
Mozart first came into this " breathing world," and
a fit nursery it is for his romantic genius.

The aspect of Munich, like that of Vienna, is
extremely *white ;* the new buildings with which the
former city is adorned have a dazzling brilliancy in
this respect that is painful to the sight, and satis-

factorily accounts for the prevalence of wearing spectacles.

Until of late years Munich has had the reputation of being the best place for the study of dramatic singing in Germany; but that was during the life-time of Winter, who was here the capell-meister; but now it is not clear whether Prague or Berlin may not contest the point of supremacy. The opera in this city has sustained two irreparable losses; the first in the death of its excellent composer Peter von Winter, and the second in that of Mademoiselle Vespermann, his best pupil, and one of those lavish productions of nature, a real singer. That the old Winter should have been gathered to his fathers when full of years and honours is not surprising. Every one who knew him speaks well of him : at a sale of his musical effects which took place a short time ago, the slightest remembrance that could be procured was eagerly grasped at. Winter was a tall man, with rather an austere cast of countenance; his manners were what the Germans expressively term *grob* (something between surly and deficient in *politesse*), but under this rough husk he had all the friendliness and sincerity which characterize his countrymen. It was his practice, as it is that of the best German composers,

especially those who are also chapel-masters, to devote some time of each day to the instruction of
girls who are intended for public singers ; and this
is done, not by *dinning* one or two songs into their
heads, but by first making them musicians, able to
read, execute, and comprehend at sight, and afterwards by making them study the sentiment and expression the composer intended to convey. In
many of the little quiet German towns through
which I have passed, the sound of young students
at their *solfeggi*, consisting of intervals direct and
inverted in every possible variety, have met my
ear, with the pleasant assurance that *they* were not
beginning to learn music at the wrong end. Mademoiselle Vespermann fell a sacrifice in her twenty-
first year to the blunders of an ignorant physician,
who negligently allowed a simple disorder to become a malignant one. Her genius for music was
so decided, and so passionately did she devote herself to her art, that in songs of pathos and tenderness she appeared to live only for the beautiful
melody. This charming creature must have felt
that, in being the organ through which the most
exquisite feeling of Mozart and Winter could be
perfectly communicated, she was only " a little
lower than the angels ;" and to a singer who feels

the real dignity of her calling, such should be the only acceptable ground of praise. The memory of Mademoiselle Vespermann is affectionately cherished throughout Germany, and her performance spoken of with enthusiasm.

On inquiring after the public performances in Munich, I received intimation of some music by Weigl (author of the Schweitzer Familie, and a Viennese composer of reputation on the Continent) to be performed at the Schweigerisch Volks Theatre, a little wooden building situate in one of the open squares, and not much better than a show-booth at a fair. The sound of the band, which made its way to the outside, did not tempt me to pursue my original design, and I turned into the magnificent church of the Jesuits, where a very good musical service repaid the disappointment. It was the festival of St. Aloysius, and it was predicted that there would be some good singing and a fine illumination. I found the prediction true with respect to the music, which consisted of a litany composed in the ancient style, and broken into several movements, or separate motetts; they were sung by a large choir and totally unaccompanied; a director gave the time, and the signals for the *crescendo* and *diminuendo,* and this service was upon the whole more delicately performed than any public church-music I have yet heard in Germany. One favourable circumstance for the music was that the crowd was perfectly quiet, and every one was fully occupied in contemplating the blaze of candles and the glitter of the altar. The organ bursting in upon the conclusion of the voices, produced a fine contrast; the player is a smooth one, and the instrument possesses the softest and roundest diapasons, or what is equivalent to them. In this church the Abbé Vogler was formerly organist. In the management of the organ the best German players are, with all their readiness in fugue, deficient in two or three important points; in a close they are too abrupt, and do not allow the tone to die away by degrees into original silence; they are unacquainted with our cathedral effects, and also with the proper mode of using the organ in choral music, as we are behind-hand in the use of the pedals and the building of those vast and voluminous toned pipes to which they give utterance. A celebrated German musician, who had visited England, declared that he could not relish the Messiah of Handel in his own country, after hearing the great effect which was produced in London by the use of the organ in the choruses. I was pleased to find that among the musical world in Munich and in other parts of Germany the fame of Handel (or Hayne-del, as they pronounce his name without the broad A) is rising on a solid basis, and that he is considered a model of the ecclesiastical style even by Catholics, for whom Haydn and Mozart have done so much. The works best known here are four—the Messiah, Judas Maccabeus, Samson, and Alexander's Feast; and the first is preferred without the additional accompaniments by Mozart.* The Germans are hardly aware how much their countryman was indebted to the English for that perfection of his taste in church-music of which he has left such enduring monuments. Handel came into England a fugue-writer of the most astonishing flow and power, well skilled in the Italian style of melody, with a poetical genius, and other natural advantages ; but it was in his retirement at Cannons, and in his intimacy with the writings of Tallis, Bird, and Purcell, that he ripened and matured his church feeling.

One of the peculiarities which strike a stranger in walking the streets in Munich, is the deep hum

* It is curious that the people for whose enjoyment these additions were expressly made should be the first to discard them.

which assaults his ear as he every now and then passes a beer-house. These places generally have a public room open to the street; and in the room, which is narrow, and retires backwards fifty feet or more in depth, there are crowds of men and women from Monday morning to Saturday night, who are generally all talking at once.

The "dolce fa niente" is much cultivated in Munich, at least it is so in the summer-time. The students here are a remarkable body; so unfettered by custom or prejudice in the mode of wearing their habiliments, that no possible extravagance in that respect would excite remark.

For the benefit of the strollers and holiday-makers in Munich, bands play twice a week in the open square of the king's palace, which both for look and accommodation may vie with the Palais Royal in Paris. Here, while the cooling luxuries of lemonade and ice are imbibed, there is a regale of excellent instrumental music. An overture in E minor attracted my attention from the brilliancy of execution and expression with which the trombone players accomplished some most unwieldy passages for their instrument. The faces of the performers appeared as if animated by a prophetic fury, and their distended cheeks would have

reminded one of the fat-faced cherubim sometimes
seen on a church organ, only that they were older,
redder, and accompanied by a " jutting *friz* " of
mustachio that cast a shade. Their enthusiasm, and
the earnestness of their manner, were delightful, as
those qualities always lead to excellence.

The opera-house at Munich is, like others I
have mentioned, in the neighbourhood of beautiful
gardens; for its internal embellishments and decorations, size, scenery, and above all its orchestra, it
is hardly rivalled in Berlin—certainly not else-
where in Germany. The light shed in upon the
audience is very mild and chastened, and also convenient, as it may enable some very unobtrusively
to devour an occasional surreptitious slice of baked
plum-pudding, which is usually vended in the pit
of the theatre, among other less substantial sweet-
meats. A lady of quality in London would faint
to see such frightful and odious vulgarity; but in
Munich the people are really not ashamed of any
thing but meanness and affectation. The opera
gave, during my stay, several pieces of Rossini, of
which the best was the Otello. In that composition, which contains undoubtedly some of the
chief of the author's writing, I heard the finest
individual and concerted performances of the style

that I have as yet met with in England, or out of it; and their excellence made me regret that the talents of the singers and band were not employed on a greater work. M. Fraenzl, jun., a pupil of Salieri, is the director of the music, and is himself the composer of some good operas.

Here I became acquainted with the vocal powers of Mademoiselle Schweitzer, who is a visitor at Munich from the court of Hesse-Cassel, where she is chamber-singer. The voice of this young lady, who was the Desdemona, is extremely sweet and powerful; her taste and intonation were also good. The manner in which she sang the Pregheira in four flats in the last act, which is a sweet *cantabile* movement, with a breathing accompaniment of wind instruments, convinced me of her talent. Mademoiselle Schweitzer presented the phenomenon of a graceful and attractive woman on the stage, though shorn of one of her natural legs, and supplied with a substitute of cork. I was indebted for this piece of history to one of the people of the opera, who thought the dexterity of her carriage worthy of observation.

Among the singers of this establishment are also a bass, M. Stadacher, whose style is far smoother and not so *staccato* as is generally the case with

that class of voices; and an excellent tenor, M.
Bayer, who displayed good feeling and discretion
in his performance.

Rossini has in this opera, in order to display the
compass and flexibility of his hero's voice, made
Roderigo ascend in some parts of the music to a
most unromantic and unmanly height, which did
not fail to create a laugh in the audience, though
that effect was undesigned by the composer.   It
is unfortunate for the *libretto* of Rossini's opera
that one cannot forbear the recollection and association of Shakespear's tragedy, the deep feeling of
which might only be expressed by the genius of a
Mozart; and on seeing the regular and unvarying
uniformity of plan upon which the *finales* of Rossini's operas are constructed, it is difficult to witness
the metamorphosis of such a story into the common
jog trot of the stage, without a feeling like contempt
at its absurdity.   The complete precision with which
every note of the accompaniment was played, might
have satisfied the most rigorous judges; and I have
found this delicacy and exactitude of the orchestra,
in which the players show themselves in their
proper sphere as the *servants* of the voice, an admirable peculiarity in their performances.   There
is a greater weight and richness in the stringed

instruments of the Munich orchestra, than in others in Germany; and though there are fewer violins than at Darmstadt, they are better, as well as better played upon.

The public taste here is less depraved than at Vienna; but it will not do at this time of day for persons to visit either of these renowned cities in the expectation of finding a general appreciation of the highest efforts in music: the audiences, if a piece be in too elevated a style for their comprehension, show by their patience and quietness that they have the will to understand; but to be silent at the end of a scena, is in Germany tantamount to the most vehement disapprobation with us. In the choice of operas the pleasure of the greater mass of listeners is always consulted; which, however just in one point of view, does not precisely agree with the aristocracy of science, and it has caused the amateurs to withdraw themselves into private societies, where they may pursue their own tastes without interruption. Of these societies there exist all sorts, even to the humble style of popular songs. The old Italian madrigals and glees, written for two tenors and two basses (a beautiful mixture for unaccompanied music, when the parts are well distributed), are in the greatest favour; and they are generally most delightfully performed, on account of the marvellous nicety of ear which *educated* German singers possess. The baron Von Poissl, director of the royal concerts, distinguishes himself much for his liberality and encouragement to ingenious young artists; and he is said to have been the most earnest promoter of that talent which has caused the young girl, Scheckner, to be idolized at Berlin.

I cannot agree with Lady Mary Wortley Montague in detesting the Catholic religion because it has made some few young women shut themselves in cloisters, who might have been just as unhappy, or less conscientious, under another form or creed. In Munich it diffuses universal cheerfulness, and especially among the girls, who flutter about on a saint's day with a gaiety in their faces, which nothing but the light-heartedness of an innocent mind could give.

The churches of the continent have ceased to be places of merchandise, and are not, like the temple of Jerusalem, occupied with dove-selling and money-changing; but still they are great auxiliaries to trade : for instance, an old woman who finds a dull market for her eggs or apples, brings her stock into church under her cloak, kneels down (after having made the usual oblation of tallow to her patron saint), patters half-a-dozen prayers, and then returning finds a brisk demand, or if she does not, thinks it not her fault. But these edifices have a still more beautiful use, for in them the halt, the maimed, and the blind daily assemble to await with calmness and serenity a release from their unhappy condition. To poor creatures who thus find consolation, the place may literally be called mother-church.

The architecture and internal appearance of the cathedral is not so elegant and symmetrical as that of the Jesuits' church; indeed the former, with its great heavy square pillars, has little to recommend it to the dignity of its appellation but size. The building is, however, favourable to sound, and some parts of the choir are worthy attention, particularly a tomb in bronze and black marble, consecrated to the memory of the emperor Louis the Fourth of Bavaria. The design and execution of this piece of art are alike excellent; the groups of figures about it are beautifully disposed, and there is a sombre deep tone in its colour that, to my mind, well harmonizes with the solemnity of the event it commemorates.

Catholic music flourishes in Munich because the

abominations of the Scarlet Lady are unceasing in
that city; and there is perhaps no place in which
the Pope, were he to leave Rome, might sooner
domiciliate.   One of the greatest musical curiosities
to be heard in their church performance, was the
accompaniment of Gregorian tones, in a manner
which I believe to have been hitherto unimagined
in any other part of the world.   Some of these
melodies were taken as *canto fermo* subjects, and
accompanied with three vocal parts in free song,
and with very florid orchestral additions.   I found
much musician-like skill in the treatment of this
idea, but am not prepossessed in favour of the taste
which could countenance this extravagant union of
styles that are void of all assimilation.   The
Gregorian tones should be preserved as they were
in the time of the elder monks, severe and awful :
these Gothic melodies are the only unclothed tunes
which are welcome to a musician's ear in that state;
on their rude sublimity, which contains the foundation of church harmony, have Handel and Leo
piled their glorious superstructures—habitations
fit for the gods.

In the cathedral I heard Haydn's mass in B flat,
No. 8, performed as usual with a full band.   The
choruses struck me as being very dignified in their

effect, but many movements were played in a time utterly distinct from that which is generally received in London as the correct one. The Benedictus, which is a soprano solo, with an *obligato* accompaniment for the organ, was taken much too fast; but it is more likely that the priests might be blameable for hurrying the music, than that the director misunderstood its character. In the last-mentioned piece, though not well sung, there was opportunity to observe the mastery of Haydn, and his extraordinary skill in every mode of combination; and though the damning fault of an incorrect time was committed, I found plenty of leisure for admiration. The soft stops of the organ blended charmingly with the stringed instruments; but the organist was rather deficient in taste, and his playing made me lament the polished and exquisite manner in which I have heard the same thing executed on a pianoforte in England. The Agnus Dei, with the expression of the words " dona nobis pacem," were well sung; but it is so difficult to preserve entire silence in these spacious buildings, that the fine subsiding of tone, the delicacy and refinement necessary in this sort of music, is greatly injured. Every time the host is elevated, the priests ring a large bell so violently, that it shatters

the nerves, and frightens one out of the agreeable
trance into which the mind is lulled. This is the
only drawback (though a great one) to the pleasure their services give in the hearing.

A ballet, with very pretty music by Cramer of
Manheim (probably a relation to the well-known
professors of that name in London) was produced
at the opera-house. The music of this species of
entertainment is generally, on account of the solos
it contains, favourable for forming a judgment on
the talents of individual performers; and it introduced me to a very clever artist, though one not
stationary in Munich, M. Hom, who is a violin-
player out of the school of Spohr. In an adagio
movement played by this gentleman, in the course
of the music I found excellent taste, and a tone
which reminded me of the sweetness of Spagnio-
letti. His bowing was also free and graceful, and
like that of a master. There is something certainly absurd and contemptible in employing impassioned melodies, full of meaning and tenderness,
to accompany balancing and feet-twirling; and it
becomes very ludicrous when, to a solemn blast of
trombones and horns, such as might prepare us to
wait in silent dread the sentence of an oracle, the
dancer, for some mysterious and inscrutable purpose,

slowly and deliberately raises her limb to an altitude as little consistent with grace as dignity. There is, in general, in the German dancing, more of the picturesque, more of graceful attitude, than of *pirouette;* and the style does not encroach so much on the province of the tumbler or posturemaster as that of France.—The scenery at Munich is extremely well painted, and always descends from the top of the house with rapidity and unerring certainty.

Before I have done with this admirable orchestra, the name of Baermann, a distinguished clarionet-player, must be mentioned, who formerly visited London; and in the softness of his tone, and the grace of his style, may be found the counterpart of Willman. That lovely instrument, the clarionet, was surely destined for Mozart, for its tones breathe nothing but tenderness and affection.

Among the other artists whose names deserve record, there is Moralt on the violoncello; Boehm on the flute; Rauch on the horn; each of the most admirable in his kind.

It is a great convenience that each seat in the pit of the opera may be locked up until it suits the proprietor of the evening to occupy it. The military and the students are privileged to a cheaper entrance of the house than other persons.

It is not the custom in Munich for the inhabitants to dine much at their own houses, but they indulge their gulosity with considerable vigour at the various hotels. In the south of Germany the dinner-hour is universally one o'clock; and as the breakfast barely justifies its etymology, being a most etherial meal, an appetite is seldom wanting at that hour. A great proportion of the guests at these public tables are officers in the army, generally fine and intelligent looking men, whose overgrown shaggy mustachios disguise much good nature, and are only the semblance of fierceness. Then comes the cook's ordeal; and a German cook is an artificer so dexterous in the occult refinements of his art, so delicate in his flavours, so profound in his combinations, that the eater shall experience no malign results in the concoction of any dish in which his subtle hand hath been employed. The courses follow one another in slow but numerous succession, and the conversation of the company, which at first commenced *pianissimo*, soon, under the influence of generous fare, becomes gradually louder as the talkers increase: at last, those who have the misfortune to be engaged in some knotty

argument or metaphysical discussion, are obliged
to halloo at the top of their voices with a most
harmless but amusing violence. When talking
earnestly upon a subject in which they are interested, the Germans roll out their fine, rough,
energetic words with infinite gusto. All this time
the mädchen (generally a pretty girl, who assists in
serving the guests individually) acts as a mode-
rator of the asperities of dispute; she insinuates
her gentle form, craving attention to some fresh
cates or dainties, or "lucent syrops tinct with cin-
namon," and generally receives in return from the
men a sly embrace or extempore compliment, or
from the women some approval of her well-chosen
dress: and this familiarity, which results entirely
from a benevolence of disposition, never degenerates
into grossness on the part of the superiors, or impudence on that of the menial. Human nature is
a very pleasant and good-natured thing in Bavaria.
I have thought it necessary to panegyrize the German cooks on account of the vivacity and mental
activity which their dishes leave to the eater, who
is after them never more cogitabund, more luxu-
riant for a sonnet or other piece of off-hand eloquence, and they sufficiently disprove that it is
alone "spare fast that with the gods doth diet."

It may serve as a characteristic anecdote of the German dilletanti in music to relate, that having some business with an ambassador, a domestic ushered me into the chamber of audience, where I found the secretary of that accomplished diplomatist, having thrown aside his papers and documents, standing in his shirt over a violin concerto of Mayseder, and labouring hard at its passages. It was evident he did not expect visitors. Having therefore apologized for receiving me in that airy dress, which I presume he had selected during the warm weather for a greater freedom of his bow-arm, he laid down his instrument, and retiring into an inner chamber, came forth in a morning-gown, and settled my business with perfect coolness and composure. A rencontre of this kind is so completely opposed to the formality and ceremony which is naturally expected in official people, that it upsets one's gravity for the instant, but upon maturer reflection it should produce admiration at that indifference to vulgar prejudices and decorum which does not sacrifice a tasteful employment, or a buoyant costume, for the risk of being surprised in a lapse of dignity.

The itinerant musicians in Germany, who go about the country in small bands, like wandering troubadours, are a class so clever and eminent in their way as to deserve notice. For a few florins these poor fellows will amuse you with such an exhibition of tone and skill as would set up an English artist of the first water. They are a set of poor but merry companions, with as little discord in their social intercourse as disturbs the harmony of their instruments; happy in spite of threadbare coats, and sunburnt, weather-beaten faces, but with a gentility of mind (owing to their acquaintance with music) much superior to other people of their *caste.*

A friend invited me to an evening concert, in which were performed the overtures and various pieces from the Don Juan and Clemenza di Tito of Mozart, excellently arranged as sestetts for two clarionets, two bassoons, and two horns; there was not power enough for the full pieces, but the airs pleased me extremely, being blown with so subdued and mellow a tone as might have been borne in a small room. This *harmonie musik,* as it is termed, is a species entirely of German cultivation, and I suspect that the wrath of old Dominico Scarlatti against wind instruments might be appeased, were he to hear how skilfully they are tempered. One of the performers gratified me with a piece of sentiment which I did not expect from a person of his appearance; after playing a tender air from an opera of Mozart, he said, " I think the composer means that the lady feels pain here," placing his hand on his heart.

The present king of Bavaria, Maximilian Joseph, is animated by a very praiseworthy desire to concentrate in his capital all the most celebrated works in painting and sculpture; and he has succeeded in his design to so eminent a degree, that it is probable Munich will soon become the haunt of artists of all descriptions and countries. The Pope, who loves his Bavarian majesty, has, it is said, withdrawn solely in his favour the absolute prohibition which he had issued with respect to the removal of ancient marbles and other works of art from Rome. The picture gallery, as it now stands, contains the spoils of the formerly famed collections of Düsseldorf, Zweibrücken, and Manheim; and though Dresden may boast *more* pictures, yet in the excellence of their classification, and in their disposal with respect to light, as well as in the intrinsic worth of the works themselves, I should prefer Munich; certainly, in the first two respects, if I am inclined to waver in the last. It is not certain whether or not difficulties might attend an artist's request of permission to copy; but for a visitor who wishes to enjoy the pleasures of the gallery, all that is required is, that he render his person at a reasonable hour under the arcade of the palace garden, and by raising his hand to a bell, and giving it an indifferent jerk, a soldier will attend him, who will, without fee or reward, conduct him to the objects of his desire. The form of writing his name is not even requested.—In spite of the exquisite pleasure it gives the eye to look at one glance through a suite of rooms, in length about four hundred feet, lined with gorgeous colours, there must be with many, I am convinced, (in their *back-ground* sensations) some secret repinings at the shortness of hours and days, and their consequent incapacity to do justice to all of the ideal and beautiful that is collected in that space. It is not as in the exhibition of our Royal Academy, where the visitor at once walks up to Turner, or Wilkie, or Sir Thomas Lawrence, without troubling himself to cast his eyes to the right or left; in the Munich gallery one is really *hustled* by the crowd of thoughts to be found in every direction, and among more than nine hundred pictures, half of which at least deserve to be well examined and greatly admired, it is not agreeable to find the attention so much overmatched as a shorter residence in the city than of several months would make it. I do not know whether the inclination be monstrous, or whether it be sanctioned by any grave authority, but how delightful would it be to abstract a certain portrait by Vandyke from the throng, and to place it alone in a private apartment, where, by perpetual conning, one might become acquainted with its minutest and most delicate touches. This is the idea of an individual as to the *conjugal* fidelity which should be preserved (at least for a whole morning) to one good picture, pure and undefiled, instead of wandering with a wanton eye through a whole bevy of them, and neglecting to pay that mental homage which a great master demands.—The Munich gallery is not rich in the Italian school, but of Rembrandt, Reubens, Vandyke, Murillo, and Velasquez, and particularly of the animal painter, Franz Snyders (who is as great in the fury of his maddened and ensanguined boars and dogs as the others are in the expression of human beings) there is of the rarest.

Much credit is due to M. von Dillis, the keeper of the Munich gallery, for the very pretty and tasteful manner in which the catalogue is made out; the language of it, which is extremely simple, frequently conveys the picture almost as forcibly to the mind as the thing itself. In some places, in two or three words, we have a whole story ; in others, the attention is unobtrusively directed to the main beauties of the artist. I hope two or three specimens may not be unacceptable.

Of Both. * " Eine Landschaft mit hohen Felsen, Bäumen, und Wasserfall. Reisende werden von Räubern angefallen."

Of Hooghe. † " In Einer von der Sonne beleuchteten Stube, sitzt eine Frau mit einem Buch."

Of Reubens. ‡ " Von der Jagd ermudete, und in einem Wald eingeschlafene Nymphen der Diana werden von Waldgöttern beschlichen.

Of Rembrandt. § " Brustbild eines Türken. Sein Turban ist mit Federn, Perlen, und Diamanten geziert."

As the gallery is always open on Sundays, it is usually resorted to between mass in the morning

---

* A landscape with high crags, and trees, and a waterfall. *Travellers are attacked by robbers.*

† In a chamber *illumined by the sun,* a lady is sitting with a book.

‡ The nymphs of Diana, *tired with the chase, sleep in a wood, and are surprised by the Satyrs.*

§ Portrait of a Turk. *His turban is ornamented with feathers, pearls, and diamonds.*

and the opera in the evening, and the day is thus not unpleasantly divided. There is an equally fine collection of sculpture, as easily accessible as the picture gallery, but I did not visit it.

In the opinion of the musical people here, there is no operatic writer at present living in Germany whose natural gifts have been more abused than those of Spontini. They are right in saying that the French have spoilt what was originally good in this composer. Every fresh opera which was intended by Spontini to make a sensation among the Parisians had more horns or trombones than the last; and to carry this excitement to a higher pitch of the *frappant*, he in one of his compositions introduced the Cyclops at work, each hammering on a gong; a very laughable mode of being original, as, if degrees of noise constitute those of excellence in music, what dire explosion will it be that gives the *ultimatum* of the art, and decides what is to be considered as its perfection.? In a composer who, like Spontini, was capable of imitating Gluck, the extravagance is less pardonable than in a mere adventurer. Of these tricks which lower the intellectual quality of music (as if its expression could really be heightened by pieces of stage effect) one is recorded of Sarti, who actually caused cannon to be fired during certain pauses of a Misererere, composed for the Russians. Such devices, however they may succeed at first, will not attain their object a second time, and may so cure themselves; but there must be as much effrontery required to exercise them as was possessed by the celebrated French preacher, who, having set before his hearers with great eloquence the terrors of the last judgment, described the Omnipotent surrounded by his angels, and dwelt upon heavenly joys and infernal agonies, while they listened with rapt attention, suddenly caused a trumpet to be blown (which he had preconcerted), and the congregation were thrown into a great panic, naturally concluding that it was the sound of that trump of which they were so earnestly thinking. The musician may however (like Rousseau from his mad sinfonia, and Dr. Busby from his oratorio for three orchestras) escape from the performance of his composition, and if he be inclined to try fanciful experiments, I think it is the most sensible plan he can adopt.—Some specimens of the English composers are now for the first time appearing here in numbers, and the work might be, if properly conducted, such as to raise the character of the English as composers to that degree of esteem in which our old cathedral masters richly deserve it should be held, and to rescue us from the imputation we enjoy abroad, of not being able to get beyond a ditty. This publication, which consists exclusively of vocal compositions, confounds all styles and names, ancient and modern, and it is evidently conducted by one who does not know where to place his hand upon our most valuable performances in church music and madrigals. Morley, M. P. King, and Webbe are classed together in it, as if those composers could convey any idea of the truly unrivalled skill in vocal canons and other pieces of learned counterpoint with which Purcell and his compeers have immortalized their names. When Dr. Boyce's great collection of our cathedral music is well known in Germany, then, and not till then, will the Germans know what masterly invention, both as to science and feeling, have originated in our country.

The English Gardens in Munich are every evening thronged by parties of visitors, each of whom may thank that benefactor of mankind, Count Rumford, for the change of a marshy uninhabitable spot of ground into one of the most luxurious kind. A monument to this nobleman, placed in the gardens, reminds the stranger of his obligation. The only objectionable thing in their arrangement (to my taste) is the violence and impetuosity of the stream which runs through them, and which, for such a place, should look clear, and run lazily rather than convey the thought of danger by its swiftness.—The university youths, who resort to the gardens in companies of half-dozens, are generally the most notable persons on the evening promenade ; they have a swaggering and assured look, but are withal frank and obliging in their manners and disposition. They appear to dispute with the military the smiles and favour of the ladies. A student of the university in Munich will not serve as a specimen of the same class in Vienna, Berlin, or Leipsic ; the former is a much more romantic and extravagant being : he makes his appearance in public thus—in a loose frock coat, from the pocket of which protrudes the end of his long tobacco-pipe ; his head is surmounted by a little cap (a mere apology for a covering, and only useful in returning the recognitions of his friends) ; his hair flows thickly down his back ; he wears an open shirt-collar ; and the cut of his mustachios and beard remind one of the taste of the cavaliers of Charles the First's time. Among seventeen hundred youths it is not to be supposed that this

fashion is universal; but yet it is sufficiently prevalent to make a decided feature in the appearance
of the inhabitants. There is not much of gallant
or deferential behaviour on the part of the men
towards the other sex, at least such conduct is not
visible in public, the Bavarian ladies being always
left and abandoned in their walks to the society of
their female friends ; and the charge of uxorious-
ness, or too great fondness, seems to be as much
scouted in Munich as it was formerly scoffed at in
England.

I have made frequent excursions out of the city
on a holiday, to witness the sports and amusements
of the country people, who on these occasions collect in a large field, where accommodations for
dancing, drinking, and other recreations are provided. Waltzing is the favourite, and indeed the
only dance here used ; and it is extremely amusing
to watch the intent gravity on the faces of the
nymphs as they are supported round the circle in
rapid revolutions by their admiring and faithful
swains. A person who reasoned from experience
and analogy might be led to apprehend, on
viewing the deadly paleness which some of the
wenches exhibited, that a catastrophe was at hand
which would render him no satisfaction in being

present at as a spectator. Men whose age no longer allows them to make themselves interesting to the girls, and who have given up all hope of being patronized as partners in dancing, betake themselves with great vigour to the enjoyments of *swinging;* and though their hearts no longer vibrate with youthful emotion, they yet find some consolation in making their entire bodies vibrate still more enormously. I have seen men of fifty years old and upwards enjoying their undulations with the boisterous screaming pleasure of a young girl at a fair. Among the very old who have abjured these volatile delights, I expected to find *cats-cradle* and *see-saw;* but this was not the case; the more grave and sober employment of drinking absorbed their faculties. Every one at these times resolves to be happy, and as it has been said, it is easier to take down than to get up, the aged find a sedentary happiness just suited to their capacities. The peasantry of Bavaria are extremely gay and enjoying; in the whole territory I have not met with a single beggar, or any one who did not look well fed and clothed.

The celebrated mass of J. N. Hummel in E flat was tried under the direction of the elder Fraenzl, by a very large vocal and instrumental band, pre-

viously to its being brought forward on a festival.
I have never been better pleased with a modern
work in church music than with this admirable
composition, and the author has shown so much
invention and beauty of design in its construction,
as to place him among the first writers for the
church now living.   Hummel is esteemed in Germany to have a greater clearness in his part-writing,
more definite and well-digested ideas, than any
modern composer, and this point of preference is
well founded.   The introduction to the mass in E
flat is so exquisitely disposed for the orchestra, the
accompaniments have such a flow of melody, and
support the vocal parts with such a subdued mur-
muring on the strings, that it is difficult to know
which should attract the greatest share of attention, voices or instruments.   There have been few
writers since Mozart who can produce this kind of
effect upon the hearer.   The fugues at the " *In
Gloria*," and in the " *Dona Nobis*," are master-
pieces of contrivance.

Before my departure from Munich I enjoyed an
evening of quartett playing at the residence of an
officer in the army, who is a distinguished amateur.
The playing of M. Hom confirmed my first im-
pressions of his excellence on the violin ; he per-

forms difficult passages with brilliancy and effect, and though he might be thought scarcely equal to the creation of astonishment, he can achieve enough for music. I was informed that the fine quartett of Mozart in D minor (which was played during the evening) was written by that composer under great mental depression, his wife being at the time under the actual pangs of her confinement. This history of a celebrated work is worth preservation.

It is between Munich and Vienna, when he loses its influence, that the traveller first becomes fully sensible of the benign interference of the Prince of Tour and Taxis in the horses and carriages of Germany; and as he mounts into an ordinary and lumbering *diligence* (in default of passengers half baggage-waggon) he deeply laments that no other illustrious potentate will undertake for his more speedy consignment from one city to the other, than in six day's time, the sad term of imprisonment which the people of the post-office promise. If he enter upon his incarceration on Monday at twelve o'clock, he will " *make* " Vienna, as the sailors would say, on Saturday evening; and it will make the difference of a half day more should he choose to proceed to Passau, and from thence embark on the Danube.

As there is no very great communication between the capitals of Bavaria and Austria, the road is barren of inns other than *cabarets* and beer houses, at which is to be found but lenten entertainment, and the forlorn *voyageur* must be content to appease his hunger with a crust, and allay his thirst with a draught of poor liquid, as all ideas of dinners and suppers (those celestial respites to the tedium of ever rolling onwards) would be the dreams of a distempered fancy—the wildest and most unsubstantial of imaginings, mocking the appetite. The reader might smile if this complaint of the want of inns were to proceed from a solitary rover in the back woods of America, or from Mungo Park in tracing the source of the Niger; but as proceeding from one who had no ambition to encounter other than European conveniences in travelling, it will doubtless awaken his gravest sympathies. Daylight never broke without hope of soup upon a merrier party than inhabited the diligence in my journey to Passau; and considering that we had only, in three days, made prize of a solitary dish of veal, our vivacity was surprising.

The Bavarian women are celebrated for their innate kindness and goodness of heart; and there is a saying with respect to them, which has grown in

some parts of the country almost proverbial—
" Sie werden nichts abschlagen,"—" they will
refuse nothing." Whether such an observation
may be borne out in fact in its widest application
I presume not to say; but their friendly natures
are sufficiently evident. A young opera-singer of
Munich, who travelled with me, having worn himself out by excess of joking and laughter during
the day, became sleepy in the evening, and not
occupying a corner of the coach, found his head
rather inconvenient; a Bavarian lady, who sat next
to him, protesting that she could never sleep in a
coach, surrendered her place to him, and in a few
minutes his head was recumbent on her shoulder,
his arm round her waist, and he slept profoundly.
When the coach stopped to change horses, I
walked with my musical friend to view the ruins of
a little Gothic church in the moonlight; and on
asking him if he was acquainted with the lady on
whose shoulder he had slept so well, he replied,
" I have never seen her before—but we do these
things for one another in Bavaria."

Up to Brennau the route is not very attractive,
except that in the early dawn we came upon an old
Roman encampment, to which we ascended to
stretch our legs and snuff the fresh morning air.

The road here is very picturesque; it winds along with heights on one side, and on the other a deep ravine, through which rushes a narrow mountain-stream with much violence. A single horseman, wrapped in a grey cloak, slowly walking his beast up this road, did not injure the lonely appearance of the landscape.

The *conducteur* of our machine was the surliest bear that I have ever met with in that trustworthy and responsible situation: his enormous bulk, and the red pimples on his face, showed him naturally of a sanguine and feverish temperament; and this irritability of constitution was not allayed by intense heat of the weather, and two or three little cross accidents—such as having unexpectedly to unpack the whole of the baggage (a labour only to be compared to unlading the hold of a ship, and discharged with an infinite variety of execration) and having to run five miles under a fervid noon-day sun to fetch fresh horses, one having fallen dead, and the other being disabled by the sultry weather. These animals we had received fresh at Brennau; they came out in the pride of their strength, lashing their long tails, and stamping with such fury on the paved stones as the flies tormented them, that the place rang with the sound. After a drive of twenty miles through a dreadfully uneven road (not the regular one to Passau, but a cross-road) there was a sad contrast; one of them fell, and though life was not quite gone, it was painful to see him unable to lift his nose out of the dust as he was dragged along by a crowd of clowns.

From noon this day, and during the greater part of the night, we travelled almost uninterruptedly through an immense forest, not kept in that trim, orderly manner in which many of the German woods are, where there is an eye to business, and where the underwood being well cleared away, the stems of the trees allow the sight to penetrate to a great distance, but where Nature had produced and reproduced for years without hindrance or obstruction. Such a wild country might fitly be imagined the haunt of banditti; and as our company was now reduced to three (occupying a small double-bodied carriage) we could more appropriately indulge such a thought. Alas for romance, and the lovers of adventure, the people have become so uninterestingly honest, that there is neither shag-eared villain nor beetle-browed assassin to be met with; and one's dormant prowess is not called into play in a single conflict. To any one who has read Smollett's powerful story in Count Fathom of the

murdered guest, a little beer-house by the road-
side, standing in the gloom of a wood far apart
from all human habitations, would convey a complete idea of the loneliness of his forester's abode.

As on the second evening, we turned out of the
sun-baked vehicle at this place to quench our thirst.
I could not be insensible to the confluence of romantic incidents before me, though at the time I
might have forsworn the experience of them for a
good supper and bed. Thunder, which had been
threatening all the afternoon at intervals, now gathered its force into one dense black cloud, which
might be seen in the distance with some of the sun's
gold still upon its edges; the rain, in slow and
heavy drops, promised us shortly a deluge; the
grasshoppers or crickets were singing a loud song ;
and the trees, "those green-robed senators of mighty
woods," lost their friendly and cheerful daylight
aspect, and their broad shade looked mysterious
and awful. The rude, dilapidated furniture of the
miserable house of refreshment would hardly have
induced any one, though thunder or worse were out
of doors, to encounter a night within it. Two or
three boors sat at a rough bench, silently drinking
their beer, while the hostess was in an inner room
on one side, playing cards with a favoured subaltern

officer. These simple employments seemed to our excited imaginations full of treason and robbery; and an old wide staircase, which led into the public room, prognosticated nothing but pitfalls and secret trap-doors for the unwary traveller. We found here, however, no daggers but in the eyes of a pretty servant girl; no poison, but in a drink of deadly beer: and having resumed our seats in the carriage, as we passed on the thunder passed off, and we arrived at Passau about four o'clock in the morning, where having routed up the landwoman of the Blackamoor's Head, we betook ourselves to repose.

The old town of Passau is remarkable for its cathedral, its very pretty maidens, and its old contra-puntist Seytl, a scholar of Albrechtsberger. There is little else to attract in it, except its bridge over the Danube, where the inhabitants collect to watch the boats and rafts as they descend from Ratisbon, and to gaze at the animal curiosities which are landed there weekly for a few hours before they are floated off to Vienna. The view from this bridge of a summer's evening is very delightful, as Passau is in the neighbourhood of some of the most enchanting scenery of the Danube. At the inn I was visited by my operatic acquaintance, for the purpose of taking a walk round the

town; he had divested himself of his travelling
dress and of his familiar gaiety at the same time,
and an embroidered coat had transformed him into
a person of solemn address and formal politeness.
The paintings over some of the doorways in this
town are occasionally extremely antique and
curious; one view of London was pointed out to
me, in which Blackfriars Bridge was represented
with a row of excellent brick houses built on the
top of it. The people of Passau think a bridge
an odd place to build upon, but then they say the
ways of the English are unfathomable, and they
are content to believe that such a plan is adopted
for the best purposes.

Here I visited a very clever and ancient professor, M. Seytl, who formerly studied the organ and
composition at Vienna, under the renowned Albrechtsberger. He is the organist of the cathedral in this town, and one of the remnants of the
Bach school of organ-playing, which is nearly ex-
tinct in this quarter of Germany. In the southern
parts of the empire there is no one who is so highly
famed for the readiness and flow of his ideas in
extempore fugue, though he is now long past the
zenith of his powers, and has turned over much
of the duty of his office to his son. The houses

in Passau are so strangely constructed, that I had to ascend to the apartments of M. Seytl by a long staircase, leading out of the street; and on being introduced to his chamber, I found an old gentleman as eager to hear musical news from England as I was willing to relate it. The face of this organist seemed to me to be cast in that large and liberal mould in which the features of Handel, Bach, and Graun are shown by their portraits to resemble each other, as if certain corresponding bodily endowments led to a certain similarity of ideas; and I could easily imagine, in looking at M. Seytl, that one of the three sat before me. He seemed greatly pleased at my anxiety to see the structure and hear the tone of his organ, and said that though he had been visited by many foreigners for that purpose, I was the first Englishman who had done so. M. Seytl asked many questions concerning our own organ-players, and also after his own countryman Johannes Baptist Cramer, of whom he seemed highly proud. As the low prayers and confessions in a Catholic cathedral are hardly ever finished, there was some difficulty in our getting to his instrument, but we at last ventured, and the unlocking of doors and the traversing of great vaulted passages that led to it, looked more like the entrance to a fortress or a prison than to a musical instrument. The organ is vast ; one gazes upwards and contemplates the immense pipes with astonishment. The absence of professed bellows-blowers prevented me from hearing the full power of the enormous instrument, but I heard the foundation stops singly, which satisfied me of its goodness. The touch is neither so deep nor so heavy as we have heard of the German organs in England. It is however much encumbered by solo stops, which are seldom in order. The manner of supplying the wind is so extremely strange to us, that it is worth record: two or more persons place themselves alternately on four large projecting logs, two of which belong to the manual and two to the pedals, and partly by their own weight, and partly by using considerable force against a bar, descend as colliers do on the river Thames in raising coals, but without one fiftieth part of their rapidity. When the logs are depressed they quickly raise their heads again, so that the labour of keeping in the wind is arduous. Our incipient bellows-blowers, M. Seytl, jun. and a friend, who had volunteered their services for my gratification, came round to us after one diapason movement, with glistening faces, or, to express the thing delicately, exuding their sudorific secretions, and declared the impossibility of their continuing their employment. By this ill-timed resignation of office I lost the opportunity of hearing the admirable Seytl finish his performance. In this organ there is among the stops belonging to the pedals a very beautiful imitation of the *violone;* the tone is smooth, and the quality of it rare. The every-day Catholic service is not accompanied on this organ, but on a small instrument placed in the choir. The cathedral itself is too gaudy and glittering in its decorations (though a Gothic structure) to give much pleasure to the beholder.

I was recommended, in passing Lintz, to visit the capell-meister and church composer, Schieder-meyer, and to view the largest organ in Germany, which that city is said to contain ; but the sudden departure of the raft did not allow me this pleasure.

VOYAGE DOWN THE DANUBE TO VIENNA.

THIS rapid river, which so well displays the justice of the poetical name bestowed upon it (Donau signifying thundering in the meadow), sends down on rafts weekly to Vienna, or into Hungary, hundreds of artificers in search of employment; and this mode of conveyance is admirably adapted for all lovers of the picturesque who are troubled with consumption of the purse, as those who choose to sacrifice personal convenience, and to brave the elements, may move forwards on their journey hundreds of miles for a few shillings' expense.

The proper way of enjoying this delightful excursion is to order a hut of planks to be put together on the raft for your own exclusive convenience; for it is impossible for one of gentle blood, though otherwise not squeamish as a traveller, to take refuge during the heat or rain in the common one, which is so crammed with old great-coats, hats, cheese, beer, and other things, that the compound of smells is villanous. The foundation of the float is of the trunks of enormous trees, so firmly attached that there cannot be the remotest fear of their separation; and when the whole cargo of planks is received on board, the surface is covered with them, and there becomes a smooth and level walk of about 150 feet in length—an extremely acceptable change for those who have been long pent in coaches. When this mass of timber is once loosened from its moorings, and in the middle of the river, it glides along swiftly and silently; and then, with heaven's breath upon one's face, may be enjoyed morning and evening views, sunsets with castles and mountains that Claude might have painted.

Soon after quitting Passau, the banks of the Danube rise abruptly on each side to an enormous height, lined with a thick forest of stunted pines or firs; and here and there, standing firmly on the peak of a rock, may be seen a solitary convent or castle, to which the entrance appears inaccessible, and all tread of human feet towards them, except by secret paths, denied. Some of these fortresses remind one forcibly of the strongholds of the enchanters, and sturdy wicked knights —those ruthless ravishers of innocent virgins with which Amadis de Gaul makes us acquainted. It is a sweet employment to stand linked on the arm of a dear and cherished friend, and to conjure up in

fancy the foregone tenants of these desolate abodes.
—The floss-meister (raft-master) and his crew, together with his passengers, must not be overlooked
in gazing at views. Our noble commander was a
short, thick-set, Dirk Haitterick-looking fellow, the
noble arch of whose nose, corresponding with a
symmetrical protuberance of his abdomen, gave
him a dignity beyond that of the office with which
he was invested : there was something gallant in the
arrangement of his dress ; whether owing to its un-
studied negligence, or to the nice adjustment of a
picturesque hat, I have not determined ; but certain it is, that the female part of the crew thought
him captivating. From habitually associating in
the elegant society of the raft, he had acquired an
urbanity and suavity of manners seldom met with
in a person of his rank ; he joked, laughed, told
stories, and answered questions—though few, unfortunately, except the pilot, understood his peculiar
and recondite phraseology. He might have possessed all the cardinal virtues, had he not displayed
on one point a touch of human weakness, and the
occasion of it was this : in a corner he nourished a
pet barrel of beer, in the administering of which
he had constituted himself sole high-priest—no one
but himself might enter that hallowed fane, no pro-

faner hand than his wield the spigot. Some reckless wights, prompted by the heat of the weather to
invigorate their alimentary canals, while his back
was turned, abstracted sundry pots; and, on ten-
dering payment, produced an explosion of wrath
that might, from its violence, have ended in a *bier*
of a more watery kind to some of the parties.

Our pilot was tall, lean, and picturesque; a fellow of infinite jest, but whose sly waggeries and
brisk sallies among the *ladies* of the company were
sometimes reproved by the captain, though upon
the whole he kept a good look-out ahead, and never
failed to stop his laughter in full career when the
sight of a crucifix reminded him he should fall to
prayers.

We had on board about fifty people, mostly
mechanic youths; but including a spruce Berlin
clerk, and a young jesuitical French priest, one who
had none of the gloomy austerity of his profession
about him, and whose dignified ecclesiastical plea-
santry showed itself on one occasion in endeavouring to thrust the foot of a young girl into one of
the puddles of water on the raft, to the destruction
of her shoe's and stocking's neatness.

The raft halts for the first night at a little village,
and the only inn where you may sleep is also in the

lower part a slaughter-house; so that if the fumes of stale meat and butcher's garbage do not obstruct your enjoyment of eating or sleeping, you may be comfortable. At this place one becomes first subject to the tiresome vigilance of the Austrian police: the sound of "aufmachen" (to make open) assaults the ear morning and evening. Keys must be surrendered, and goods and chattels overhauled, lest tobacco should be hidden in the trunks. I thought these Austrian supervisors blindly obstinate in the execution of their task, and moreover stupid, for they made no distinction between the physiognomy of an *indifferent* traveller, and the cunning look of a regular contraband trader. They have no remorse in demolishing all the order and economy of your portmanteau; and if among your books they find a favourite author, or passage to their taste, it is not that you are waiting to lock up, or that you did not request their opinion of your literature, which will make them desist from this droll stretch of power.

The first half of the second day carries you through as many beautiful scenes as any part of the journey. In many parts the turnings of the river are so abrupt, that the mountains and trees on the banks form complete amphitheatres; in others, the

dark rocky cliffs on the sides give one the idea of
riding into a cavern.   Until a few miles before the
entrance to Lintz, there is no flatness to be seen in
any of the views on the river; and except castles
and monasteries, there is not a single habitation
other than the rudest fishing huts, though here and
there are placed little chapels and altars, just in
size and shape fit for the occupation of a Newfound-
land dog.

Our ragged and jovial company, though every
ten minutes sailing through a new and beautiful
panorama, did not give them much attention.
Some twopenny editions of Walter Scott's romances
engaged a score of them; others, in spite of the
hot sun, fished inveterately for the whole day, indeed the whole three days and a half, without
catching any thing.   It might be said of the Danube, as a wag said of an unfruitful stream, that
there was a great deal of fish-*ing* there, but no fish,
in which the English language is a little bruised
for the sake of the agreeable paradox.   A lusty
young fellow, student of a military gymnasium,
and the identical scape-grace who had irritated our
noble captain by drawing his beer, this day exhibited some swimming, which, for long continuance
and the roughness of the stream with which he had

to contend, might have done honour to a Leander. The great length of the raft and the shelter of a large boat which it carried, gave him the opportunity of disrobing with great privacy and delicacy, and there was nothing in his conduct to shock the decorum of the female passengers. We were a little annoyed by the smoke of the floss-meister's cookery, which was hardly to be called intermittent. With this personage and his crew appetite did grow with that it fed on, which was lumps of seethed flesh; ever and anon a fire was lighted on a piece of baked clay, a pipkin placed thereon, and mutton inserted; and as the priests of old were allowed to keep for themselves whatever they could fish up by harpooning into the pot, so did these people regulate their diet, striking in by turns with the most perfect resignation to the decrees of Fate in its awards.

We arrived at Lintz, a fine city on the Danube, by sunset, and anchored there for the night. The bridge over the Danube is the evening walk of a whole college of priests, who strut by twos and threes backwards and forwards, as if conscious of the power they have gained over the grovelling intellects of the common people in Austria. The night's lodging in Lintz, though attended with a better supper and bed than any other of the journey, has an ill-assorted convenience with the vagrant accommodation one experiences on the rest of the journey; at this place a man may at his inn ring lustily about him, and take his ease. At supper they placed before us the famed Danube carp, a species of fish I cannot think destined by nature to pass into the human stomach, at least by the mouth: through the most artful gravies and profound seasonings it betrays its fundamental hideousness of flavour. Nor can I praise the red Hungarian wine, which is at once sweet and strong, and puts fire to the blood of the drinker. Now, although a fever is of slight consequence, provided one can eat, sleep, and walk well, as the Hungarian wine does not make this little reservation in its effects on a patient, it is perhaps wise to avoid it.

I was highly amused with the sight of a picture gallery here, such a one as might easily have been made up of the refuse of marine store shops, and select parts of the unsold chamber garniture of Saffron Hill; and the exhibitor, an old gentleman, wore so important an air of gravity in pointing out their beauties, that it might be imagined he contemplated in them an abstract of all European treasures of art.—The churches in Lintz are not handsome; they exhibit nothing in the interior but new white-wash and gilded baubles.—In the announcement of Boieldieu's opera, La Dame Blanche, the enormous list of *dramatis personæ* caught my eye with some surprise; but I soon found that it was swelled with each individual of the chorus, down to lamp-lighters and scene-shifters.

Among the low Austrian people I have found a greater disposition to cunning and chicanery than in other territories, and one instance of it happened in Lintz; a guide whom I employed to convoy me through some of the most curious edifices in the city, was so ingenious as to avoid all open doors, and to select no passages or entrances to a building but such as were double-locked and barricadoed, that by means of this elaborate progression, the value of his services, and mediation with obstinate warders and beadles might be enhanced; the artifice was however luckily discovered before he or his accomplices had received an extra *kreutzer*. This scheme is in my own experience not altogether without precedent; on going with a party to visit the palace of the Luxembourg in Paris, we held a whispering parley with the *major-domo*, who showed us that it would be clean against rules to admit us;

the man of office however suddenly relenting, with equal benevolence and bravery, beckoned us to follow him, which we did in a swift yet silent trot; yet so little real necessity was there for this exaggerated movement, that we might have stalked in to the Dead March in Saul, and have fired minute-guns without fear of interruption.

We parted from Lintz at about eleven o'clock in the morning. The floss-meister did not generally incommode us by requiring our early attendance; he could calculate his distances and times of arrival to a great nicety. In clearing the arch of the bridge at Lintz with our apparently unwieldy machine, it was manifest that a critical exactitude would be necessary; but this nice point in the navigation of the river was achieved with almost incredible skill, especially when the force of the current is considered. Four or five oars tied to short posts at the opposite ends of the raft, are the simple means of guiding it, and the watermen who work them are in their natural inclinations so exquisitely lazy, that they engage in card-playing until the raft threatens to run aground; they then rush to their posts, and pull as though they were possessed, and having once more gained the middle of the river, they are then idle again. Every time we passed a monastery the monks pushed off a boat for contributions, levied in the name of the Virgin Mary, whose effigies, accompanied by her infant's, were always carried in the boat in a sort of doll baby-house, and this exaction (it amounts to such where to refuse would be thought a crime) was the more galling to me on account of the poor work-men, who never refused their mite, though, by the look of their coats, it might have been better em-ployed in fencing out the winds of heaven from their carcasses.—The night before we reached Vienna our voyage continued long after sunset, and at length we reached a kind of pot-house close on the left bank of the Danube, which we entered with the cheering anticipation that at two o'clock in the morning the raft was to be under weigh, that unseasonable hour for sailing being selected by our devout commander and his pious pilot, wholly and solely for the sake of attending mass at a certain village. The whole of our company supped this evening at separate tables placed round one room, and I suppose that there was never out of Germany, so poor, so merry and noisy a society, and so utterly without *blackguardism* at the same time, as this was. There was no instinctive sub-ordination; we herded in different parties out of mutual convenience and delicacy ; to some it was pleasant to enjoy a dish of meat, a bottle of wine, and a bed ; to others, bread and cheese, beer, and a moonlight ramble were the agreeable thing, and we were all equally pleased and equally independent ; and I would rather enjoy another rouse with these honest lads on the Danube, to see their friendliness and frankness, the bright sides of human nature (not brought out only by the good-fellowship of meat and drink, but the same either full or fasting), than I would be at an evening party, where the silk stockings are of the most exemplary, the pantaloons of the most orthodox, and where the intellectual vigour of the conversation displayed, is but a slight compensation for the want of that moral transparency I have been mentioning.

Our host having miscalculated the time of his guests' arrival, and being disturbed in his own refection, would have made a good portrait for Mathews, of the fat, choleric German cook ; with a nightcap stuck on the back of his head, he appeared every now and then moiling and fuming from the kitchen, and exasperated to the highest degree at the inefficiency of his domestics. His daughter followed close in the footsteps of her sire, ready to assist at his slightest beck, and I know not whether it be by the force of contrast, but I have seldom seen a more lovely face and graceful form than this girl possessed, and must conclude that she was reared in this desolate region by a providential interposition, lest too many hearts should suffer.

While my noisy comrades, every one of whom seemed in motion, were chirping over their cups, I escaped from their clamour to enjoy the silence and calmness of the night without. The moon was shining full on the broad Danube; its trembling silvery surface looked placid, though it was then running swiftly as ever; the mountains on the other side the river, with their shapes ill defined in that dubious light, helped to complete the night landscape. On this spot might be enjoyed all the poetry of loneliness; the tread of one's own footsteps on the gravel, and the deep thronging of voices which sounded in that isolated dwelling, were circumstances which made the quiet and serenity of the scene more intensely felt. I have often thought that situations of this sort, which live in the memory, are best described when contemplated at a distance, as it is not easy to dissect emotions and feelings, and to paint them under the actual impression of pleasure, for the same reason that an artist who would take a view does not place himself in the centre of it. It is during night-travelling in this romantic country that one may become fully sensible of the effects which inspired Goethe with the grand idea of animating those parts of nature which are sublime even in their repose :

> " Seh' die Bäume hinter Bäumen,
> Wie sie schnell vorüber rücken,
> Und die Klippen, die sich bücken,
> Und die langen Felsennasen,
> Wie sie schnarchen, wie sie blasen."*

In leaving this place we found that the morning fog and intense cold felt on the Danube at daybreak have not been overstated. Those whose garments were delapidated resorted to the airs in La Dame Blanche, singing and beating a *tattoo* with their heels at the same time. By eleven o'clock we reached a little village to breakfast, and its name resembled the inharmonious sound Stein

---

* " But see how swift advance, and shift
  Trees behind trees, row by row ;
  How, clift by clift, rocks bend and lift
  Their fawning foreheads as we go.
  The giant-snouted crags, ho ! ho !
  How they snort, and how they blow !"
  Translation by Shelley from Goethe's Faust.

und Gremps, but whether that orthography be
genuine or not I have not means of ascertaining.
A mass was sung in the church by a crowd of
Austrian boors, the correctness of whose ears, and
a certain wild and untutored hankering after harmonies in their performance, gave me pleasure.
Within the doors of this church were kneeling,
apart from the rest of the congregation, three or
four wretched objects, the abortions of the village,
men who had been sent incomplete into this breathing world, and who made a disgusting parade of
their misfortunes.   Our floss-meister and his pilot
having enfranchised their consciences from the
thraldom of sin, we pursued our journey, and
landed about four o'clock in the afternoon within a
league of Vienna.——The famed whirlpool of the
Danube, called the Strudel, is situated in a very
narrow and picturesque part of the river, with
beetling rocks on the right hand side, surmounted
by a crucifix; but the raft is carried with such rapidity past this scene, that there is hardly leisure
to admire it; there is however not the least danger farther than wetting one's legs by a trifling rush
of water between the timbers; of which inconvenience the pilot warns the passengers beforehand,
so that it may be avoided by stepping a few paces

backwards. The summer palace of Prince Schwartz-
enberg, and the Abbey of Mölck, are two of the
most superb buildings now inhabited on the banks
of the Danube, and no description of mine could
do justice to the beauty of the situations they
occupy.—I have been the more particular (perhaps
tedious) in noting the events of this expedition
from Passau, because many are anxious to know
with how few inconveniences such a tour may be
accomplished. In my apprehension, the pleasure
of looking out on some of the grandest views,
amply compensates for two nights of indifferent
sleeping, and two days of meagre diet; but the in-
termediate rest at Lintz does not require mortifica-
tion of the flesh in either way, and one may there
indemnify oneself for abstemiousness past and to
come.

The situation of Vienna is not remarkably picturesque, at least when viewed from that point on
which it is entered on landing from the Danube.
In vain did I look for those fertile environs, those
green and shady woods, mountains, and vineyards.
which itineraries promise; but perhaps the country
may, in saying this, be rather unjustly treated, for
the driver of the *fiacre*, who was conveying two or
three of our party into the city, displayed his con-

summate skill by whipping his horses to their full speed, and at the same time keeping the off wheel of his carriage as near as possible to the edge of a precipice, so that uncertainty as to the equilibrium of the machine occupied a good share of our attention. We were silently computing at how much risk of our lambdoidal processes we might make the descent in case it were necessary.—The inquisitorial search authorized by the Austrian government into the trunks and passports of a stranger, becomes here most vexatious and annoying; it is hardly possible to proceed a hundred yards without having some formulary to discharge. At the barriers the visitor receives a paper requiring that he present himself personally within twenty-four hours before certain official people, to receive a licence for residing in the city. Before this last document is delivered to him, he must endure a course of frivolous and irrelevant questions, such as his age, religion, whether married or not, object of his journey; and, to conclude, he must, by producing a letter on a banker or some responsible person, *show* that he possesses the means of supporting himself there, or be ejected forthwith. It is not to be supposed that these tedious preliminaries are always settled without their dullness being seasoned by a

joke; the impertinence of the inquiries is sometimes well ridiculed by the most absurd answers,
evidently framed for the purpose. Thus, an English officer in the army being asked the purport of
his journey to Vienna, answered " to fish for
trout;" and as the truth of this staggering communication could not be controverted, it was received.

Vienna is a small city, thickly inhabited; its
walls enclose more men and buildings than can be
found in the same space in any other capital I have
visited. The streets are so narrow that the eye of
the passenger cannot take in the structure of the
houses, and the only places where a view of the
elegance of the buildings may be enjoyed are in
the squares. The Graben, a broad street in the
heart of Vienna, is the pleasantest part of it for a
lounge, on account of the splendour of the shops,
particularly those of jewellery and of ladies' shawls,
dresses, &c., in which it is extremely brilliant.
Most of the passages leading to the ramparts
(which latter form the evening promenade) are not
very agreeable, especially those leading from the
narrower streets, as their detestable stench is continually reminding an Englishman of the peculiarity in his conformation, a nose that discrimi-

nates. The buildings of the suburbs are not allowed to approach within a certain boundary of the city walls, and the appearance of them would be improved if they did not lie so bare to the sun. There is a want of trees about Vienna; all the gardens in the suburbs for the amusement of the public look like plantations ; the shrubs and trees appear as though they had been stuck in yesterday, but the truth is they are little and old, and do not take kindly to the soil.—From the specimens of the musical performances I have met with, there is scarcely a corner of Europe in which the taste of the operatic community can be worse. It has been said that the people of Vienna are Rossini mad, but they are not only mad for him, but mad for his worst imitators ; with good ears, they tolerate the worst of music. They out-herod Herod in their noisy and vociferous applause of their favourites : this is the system now pursued towards a lady who is in the good graces of the audience ; she receives a loud greeting on her entrance, is interrupted with *bravos* in the middle of her song, there is more applause when she has finished, and after quitting the stage she is regularly called for back to make her obeisance, and to hear fresh acclamations. Mademoiselle Lalande is clever, but she would not deserve all this if she united in her own person all the talents of all the singers from Gabrielli to Fodor, and such noisy commendation would seem more like a combination to support worthless music and a bad performer, if it were not known that the vanity of many hearers leads them to bestow it for the sake of a side-long compliment to their own discrimination and taste.—Every thing Italian is in fashion at Vienna, the language, music, and singers; and though the opera-house is a poor one seen after that at Munich, the former has the advantage (if it can be called so) of having a composer and a corps of native artists, so that the Italian opera in its original state flourishes there. Pacini is engaged as composer for the opera in Vienna. This young man is not so ideal a workman as Rossini, but he is a more punctual one, and his qualification is of much importance where crowds would die of *ennui* if their darling novelty were withheld beyond its expected time. The little theatres in the Joseph Stadt and the Leopold Stadt have each their Drechsler and Müller, who labour in their vocation to keep the public wish for the new from sinking into torpor and inactivity; and though they are like cats following their tails, always working in a circle, it is not probable there will be any complaint against them in Vienna until they stop for want of *ideas*.   A new Italian opera by Pacini, entitled Amazilia, was announced every day in the week for representation, and as duly put off, for Vienna is the only city in Germany at which this sort of finesse is esteemed; at last it was brought forth.   It was an opera of three songs, all the rest went for nothing; the composer had made some points to entrap the audience, and they were entrapped.   The heroine had in the key-stone of the opera to make the circuit of the stage in slow and measured steps to alternate *solos* on the cla-rionet and horn; she had to look pensive and in-teresting during the long symphony, which excited expectation; then came the modern adagio, full of slow notes and quick runs, and afterwards the bril-liant allegro overpowering the hearer with a torrent of passages.   All this would be very pretty if one could be kept in good humour during a whole evening by one or two good pieces, when the whole should be good; but the worst effect of this foolish toleration on the part of the audience, is, that it offers no stimulus to the composer, who of course will take little pains with a work which in a fort-night's time will be put among the theatrical lum-ber.   This taste has been imported into Vienna from Italy.—The three stars of the opera at present in Vienna are Mademoiselle Lalande, Signor David, and Signor Lablache. The young lady was born in France, but was removed into Italy whilst very young for her musical education, and she now holds the rank of member of the Philharmonic Society in Bologna. As a prima donna, Mademoiselle Lalande reminds me of Madame Ronzi di Begnis in the force and energy of her style; but, with an equality of talent as a musician and a charming person, as an actress she falls far short in the comparison. David, the first tenor, may be reckoned old for a singer; his voice is tremulous, his face effeminate, and his person thin and attenuated. In former days there was doubtless some foundation for the praise which has been lavished upon this singer by those who have visited Italy, but at present he discovers little to warrant his great fame, unless we perceive it in a style full of that *frippery* for which Crivelli and Garcia have made themselves remarkable. David has the appearance of an antiquated beauty; his throat is whitened, his features look enamelled, and, except when exerting himself in his *falsetto* to reach (at which time they are moulded into a shape something between smiling and weeping) they are immoveable. He too, like some singers of the day, has a favourite note in his voice, which he throws out with great fervour, and once or twice I could not help thinking, that had he just been shipwrecked, and was clinging to a plank in the Bay of Biscay, he could not have made more noise to hail a ship that was passing, than he did on a dry stage for the sake of Pacini's opera. David does not want feeling, if he would but in some degree sacrifice the graces instead of sacrificing to them; but there is in the modern Italian opera such a temptation to the singer to supply the melody of a song, on account of the sketchy nature of the original, that if he overshoot the mark, some frailty may be pardoned. The bass singer Lablache is a tall, stout, handsome, and good-natured-looking Neapolitan. He appeared in Amazilia as a cacique of Indians, and strode about the stage, brandishing a massive club, and burlesquing with the most extravagant action a part which would have been as contemptible as absurd if attempted to be played *seriously*. He is a good singer, but on this occasion his angry voice was like the bellowing of an enraged bull, and the assumed violence was in keeping with his gestures, and a relief to the feel-

ings of the audience. Lablache is a great favourite
with the ladies of Vienna ; the guerdon of his services has less of noisy applause in it, and more of
" nods and becks, and wreathed smiles," than that
of others.—The price of admittance into the opera-
house here is four times that of the theatre in
Munich, and the band and chorus are far inferior.
The director of the music is Weigl; this composer
takes his place in the orchestra in so plain a costume, that his jean coat appears as though it had
been doing good service in his study five minutes
before ; and it is thus proved (a fact hardly to be
believed in England) that music may be conducted
although its conductor be not invested with the
dignity of full dress.

In the summer months the Viennese gentry
forsake their hot and unairy streets, and seek fresh
gales and cooling baths in the country ; the musicians fortunately remain behind, though concerts
are not so prevalent as in winter. Vienna, like
other great Catholic cities, is seldom long without
some sight, something *out of the way* for the po-
pulace to gaze after, and I was not surprised nor
displeased in attending a midnight concert, performed on the place of the cathedral of St. Stephen, by order of the archbishop. The stillness

of the hour, and the quality of the music, which
was played in the open air, renders this occasion
an epoch in my musical adventures. The compositions given were of the very best. The overture to Weber's Oberon, an air with variations on
the violoncello, the slow movement of Beethoven's
Sinfonia in A, a Concertino of Mayseder on the
violin, and Mozart's Overture to the Zauberflöte.
In the opening of Oberon the tones of the horn
derived such purity and richness from the open
air, and such an echo from the stone flooring, as I
never before heard in any concert; but when listening in darkness, and with nothing externally to
distract, but all one's thoughts turned inward upon
the music, the perception of its beauty may be
more acute in the listener, than that the thing
itself is really better. I expected to hear Mayseder play at this serenade, but he has lately taken
upon himself the hymeneal bonds, and forsakes
the town for a pleasant dinner and evening in the
gardens of the suburbs. All the orchestral pieces
were extremely well executed, and were led with
great spirit by M. Paem, a gentleman belonging to
the Hof Capell (Royal Chapel.) The Germans
possess many violoncello players of much execution, and Bernard Romberg is the one generally

cited as being at the head of them; the fact is, that although talent is more extensively diffused in Germany, and that country produces many artists, it is less concentrated than among us. The taste of Robert Lindley is more nearly approached in Vienna than his firm hand and brilliant tone; hence the execution of Merk on the violoncello was weaker in point of articulation than might have been wished, as his feeling was good, his intonation exact, and the passages were distinct, but they were without force. I was much gratified by the performance of Merk, and should rate him higher than any of our players except Lindley; but the want of strength and pressure of the finger is his principal defect. Merk's proficiency was chiefly shown in bowing across the strings, in the delicacy of his taste, and in accurate stopping on the thumb parts of the instrument. There is perhaps too great a love of scrambling over difficulties among the artists in Vienna, who suffer that ambition to swallow up some of those energies which should be devoted to the art abstractedly. The concertino violino performed by Paem, was executed with much brilliancy and a good tone; the character of the music was of that tricksy mixture of melancholy and gaiety which is found in Mayseder's writings. For a serenade, or night concert, I should have preferred some pieces of a graver sweetness than those well-known overtures display; and the movement which to my mind harmonized best with the time and place, was Beethoven's Andante. The effect of this was charming, and it was played with true feeling and expression. The reader must imagine himself on a hot night standing among a crowd of people, who are puffing their tobacco-smoke so vigorously that he may but dimly see the moon, which is partially lighting the old spire of St. Stephen. The front of the cathedral is in deep shade, and the feeble gleam of a lamp here and there under the arch of the great entrance, serves to make the blackness beyond more palpable. If a Gothic cathedral looks solemn in the day-time, at night it looks sombre. St. Stephen behaved himself more decorously at the concert than others of the audience, who were somewhat infuriate after the Overture to the Zauberflöte, and absolutely refused to go home to their beds without a repetition of it, and the desire made a kind of reparation for the bad taste the Viennese showed in the opera-house. This was the first time I had heard Mozart played upon his own ground, the place where he lived, loved, thought, and wrote, and the occasion was one which might quicken the aspirations of a musician after the perfection of his art. Music is not like poetry, a morning pleasure ; the musician's thoughts do not *generally* flow so well at that part of the day, nor have we then the same capability of enjoying his art. It should be reserved " to make wanton the night," that we may leave a dalliance with beautiful sounds and shapes, languid but not cloyed, to fall asleep with them hovering around, and gently mixing with our last half-defined and shadowy perceptions, and then is sleep Elysium. About one o'clock after midnight I returned home, thinking how sadly Germany has within the last year or two been bereft of those who have given her treasures of music and beauty ; there are Beethoven and Winter, Fesca, Danzi, Andreas Romberg, and Weber, all dead ; as for Haydn and Mozart, who have made the very ground of Vienna sacred, they must by this time be quite incorporated with the elements.

The public concerts in Vienna generally take place in the middle of the day. The head-quarters of the musicians in the city, at which they generally assemble to lounge over the gossip of their art, is at an inn called the *Matschaker Hof*, in the Seiler Gasse: here Beethoven, before his last illness, was frequently to be found. At the time of my visit, the concertos of a celebrated English pianoforte player, which had been lately tried in Vienna, were the subject of criticism; and were condemned, on the score that the orchestral parts were badly managed: but, with all deference to high German authorities, I was obliged to demur to the judgment, for the style of scoring a concerto at present in fashion on the Continent, makes the combination of instruments too important a feature, instead of keeping them to the principal one merely subordinate and adjunct. It would be difficult to decide who should have precedence among the pianoforte players at present in this city—there are so many whose merits are, within the weight of a feather, equally balanced. Mr. C. Czerny is supreme as a pianoforte teacher and composer, and all his opinions on the subject of his instrument are received as canons. At evening parties in which a number of players meet, it is usual for each to do something on the instrument, mostly *extempore*, and the newest comer is first complimented with the seat of honour, and expected to be original and entertaining as soon as he takes off his hat. At these times I have not heard any thing very admirable elicited; but it is worthy of remark how, by an habitual practice of modulation, a person becomes enabled to pursue an idea very pleasantly and ingeniously.

The "Agnese" of Paer, in which Mademoiselle Lalande threatened to make her *last* appearance at the opera, introduced me more intimately to the talent of this lady in songs of pathos and passionate feeling; and I am glad of the opportunity of recording her genius in these particulars. Lablache also, as the distracted father, astonished me by the feeling of his singing, and the truth of his acting, and showed a wonderful change from the prodigious folly and bombast of his demeanour and singing as an Indian cacique. The first act of Paer's opera is perhaps the highest effort of the modern Italian school; it contains an elegance of melody and a richness in its scoring which show invention, and are utterly distinct from that kind which is made up upon one regular model. There are in Paer's opera, ideas worthy Cimarosa: instead of one eternally prominent part, the different characters are in the concerted music well mixed up; it contains none of those tiresome unaccompanied glees in which Rossini and his followers delight—bringing their singers in a row before the lamps in all cases of rejoicing or calamity, life or death, to go through the regular routine of outstretched hands, uplifted eyes, pressed bosoms venting their agony in triplets, or their distraction of mind in a *roulade*. I must instance, as an exquisite specimen of Mademoiselle Lalande's powers, her scena " Tutto è silenzio intorno:" the subdued natural tones of her voice, and the elegance and finish of her style, delighted me.

Lablache equalled Ambrogetti in his powerful and natural representation of Uberto, and sang his part still better, in a sweet and unforced bass voice. The scena, " Ah, si, si . . . . . . lo troverò," on the entrance of Uberto into the wood, after his escape from the mad-house, was one of the most over-powering dramatic exhibitions I ever witnessed— though I believe Lablache has not, like his prede-cessor, studied his dreadful part among the melan-choly inmates of a lunatic asylum.

But if the main incident of the story (a father whose reason gives way under the misery of losing a favourite daughter) be too affecting for public representation, how is good taste violated in mixing up with this sad spectacle the ludicrous fright of the maid who brings in the coffee; and the revolting buffoonery of Pasquale, intendente dell' Ospitale dei Pazzi, who gets his fingers pinched in the snuff-box of Uberto. Lablache never once forgot the seriousness of his part, though the prodigious absurdity of the buffo (who is a Munden in the arts of grimace and face-making), and the elaborate contortions of body and dexterous pirouettes with which he wheeled out of his way, might have created laughter "under the ribs of Death." The fault of the music is, that the best part is the first, but the anti-climax is easily accounted for by the story, which becomes gradually more cheerful and more commonplace.

The plain recitative at the opera in Vienna is not well accompanied; and I heartily wish the performer could hear the fanciful and exquisite manner in which Lindley does this at our Italian Opera-house. The chords are indeed struck upon the violoncello (without that *arpeggio* and brilliancy, the unique excellence of Robert Lindley), but their effect is tame. The pianoforte in the orchestra is more in tone like a spinet that might have been used in the time of Sebastian Bach or Handel. The front seats in the pit are, upon extraordinary occasions, occupied by some old gentlemen who have witnessed all the revolutions of the science, from the time of Mozart's supremacy to the present day. It is pleasant to see one of this class taking his place early, in all the formidable dignity of the old school, with his portentous *knocker* and dress hat and ruffles; he is pulvilled and perfumed, and smells like a "latter spring;" he has enjoyed Mozart and Paiesiello in his youth, he is learning to like Pacini against his second childhood; but notwithstanding all vicissitudes in taste, it is not disagreeable to reflect that the love of music or of enjoyment at least survives.

This morning I visited the Abbé Stadler, who was so kind as to show me the manuscript of Mozart's last and greatest work, the Requiem, which is in his possession. There is a three-fold interest about this gentleman—that he is a learned church composer, that he is extremely amiable, and that he was the young and dear friend of Mozart. If the reader choose to accompany me in this interview, he must picture to his fancy the abbé as a slight and venerable figure, rather short than otherwise, enveloped in a morning gown, and wearing a little brown wig; his hands are somewhat tremulous with age, but his face, smooth almost as an infant's, tells of a life passed in serenity; and one may soon perceive that suavity and gentleness are constitutional with him. Talk with the kind abbé of

Mozart, and he warms into rapture, tells of an inspired being, who within a short space put forth
more exquisite works than have been ever devised
in the longest life, of a being full of affection, sensibility, and sociality, who was once his intimate
and associate ; and as he lingers fondly over old
scenes, he may say, as he did to me, " All these
things have long passed away, but I am here still."
In the Abbé Stadler I saw the *real* tomb of Mozart ; and few of those who have lived in marble
for two hundred years may boast such honour as to
have their remembrance last fresh and ardent in the
warm bosom of a human being for forty. The acquaintance of the Abbé Stadler with Mozart commenced when the latter was nine years old. The
score of the original MSS. was produced, or rather
part of it, from the *Dies Iræ* to the *Sanctus* (the
rest being in the custody of Eybler, the Hof capell-
meister) : its appearance, and the melancholy history connected with its composition, which I believe every one knows took place while the author
was hurrying to the grave, filled me with a crowd of
emotions. One of them was like that which a de-
votee would experience on seeing an undoubted relic
of his favourite saint—the thin, sickly fingers that
had pressed that paper, the pale anxious face that

had been bending over it—how must Mozart have looked, and how felt, when penning the *Lachrymosa* and the *Rex tremendæ*—his being sublimating to an essence, to his fingers' ends and in his feet must he have felt the intense pleasure of creating, his mortality all the time wrestling with the deity within. No one of sensibility could have written the Requiem without a great shock to his physical strength ; he must have lived in a fever of thought, have trodden the air unclogged by " this vile body ;" nay, I think that even if a ruddy Devonshire farmer could have produced it, *knowing* what he was doing, it would have made a ghost of him. The notes are small and clear, but there is a hurry and dash in the strokes by which they are joined together, which show the ardour and completeness of the author's design. There are no alterations, and it is the first transcript of Mozart's mind. In some of the passages I thought I could discern a tremulousness in the marks, which seemed as if he apprehended life would be gone before he could make his thoughts eternal ; or did he tremble from contact with their extreme beauty, as the bee seems to do when he grapples with a flower ? The *Recordare* appears most carefully written ; the score is not full ; wherever there is a duplicate part, it is filled up by an assistant, but the figures are carefully marked in Mozart's own hand. Two observations are suggested by the sight of this work: first, how by a few strokes a great genius goes farther in the result than the most painful elaboration of thought will arrive at, and also how certain habits of thinking allow a man in the hastiest composition to defy with safety the sternest and most unrelenting criticism to find a fault, and to which indeed, were it the subject of a lecture, the professor's exordium might be, " This is perfection of its kind." The Abbé Stadler also possesses the desk at which Mozart *stood* when engaged in composition; it is a deal one, painted, but its coat is the worse for wear.

In less than forty years so completely has every bodily trace of Mozart vanished from the minds of the people of Vienna, that there is not a soul there who can even tell the place in which he was buried: by some strange accident the Abbé does not even know it. The answer to every inquiry is, " Nobody knows—the register of St. Stephen's must be consulted for the information." There is no rude memento, no sculptured stone, to indicate that the divine Mozart once sojourned in Vienna; and as for the spot of his interment, it may not be

thought too fanciful to suppose, that Earth, the
general mother, jealous of her production, has
hidden him again in her womb, lest celestial beings
should claim him as their own.   This is perhaps a
poetical apology for what is in fact a piece of
neglect everlastingly disgraceful to the Viennese,
who, I am afraid, have more joy in the pageant of
a funeral, than they have sorrow for the loss of
great men.

The Abbé Stadler showed me some lessons in
composition which Mozart had given to his niece;
and we observed the method he adopted to try her
abilities in music by first giving her a melody without a bass, then a bass without a melody, then by
degrees requesting her to add the inner parts.   I
also saw Mozart's own early exercises, some of
which consisted of canon in all the intervals (most
adroit in the seventh, that apparent contradiction),
with fugues, &c., a ground-work in harmony,
which, coupled with his fine invention, made him
the great master he was.   Mozart's *extempore*
playing was so exquisitely regular and symmetrical
in design, that it was impossible for judges who
heard him not to imagine that the whole had been
written before—which is the ultimatum of praise.
The Abbé Stadler observed, that it was impossible

to take a minuet out of a quartett or quintett of
Mozart, and not to discover that he was a great
master of fugue; but his admirable fancy was ever
found "taming its wildness to the loving hand" of
Nature. As a player, his left hand, the weakest
and most uncertain part of "human mortals,"
never missed fire when he levelled it at a passage.—
Mozart's widow, who has been married to a gentleman in Copenhagen, has lately lost her second husband: one of his sons is a musical teacher and
composer of no great eminence, the other is a merchant at Milan.

The German opera is not much patronized by
the Viennese, who doat upon those things which
are *foreign*, and despise their own good writers.
Both the Italian and German opera are played at
the same house; but the latter is considered by
the public as a mere foil to the former, and by the
managers as a mere stop-gap. Weber's Freischütz
was produced during my stay, a circumstance
which pleased me extremely, because I wished to
remark the difference between our own adaptation
and the original. The transposition of situation in
the music, and (in some parts) its alteration for our
own theatres, is not favourable to Weber. Much
beautiful concerted music is omitted among us,

particularly the last *finale*, which, with its imitations and fugued passages, is extremely good. The German singers are now so familiar with the opera, that the choruses go with a joviality and spirit beyond all imagination, for their parts have not the appearance of having been studied, and in a romantic opera it is essentially necessary that the music should flow as it were spontaneously from the mouths of the singers, leaving them to get into the thick of the scene with untaxed memories. The incantation scene is not managed with that fine accumulation of horror that it is in London; all intercourse with the fiend takes place in the decayed and hollow trunk of a tree. The devil is not allowed to appear on the Austrian stage; for priestly despotism will not allow that lovely bugbear to make his appearance before the public, lest good Catholics should get used to him, and in time begin to dandle and cocker him as they do their favourite saints, and then how would the argument of terror be weakened, which has hitherto been found so beneficial in improving people's lives and in lightening their consciences and purses.

At the smaller theatres in the Leopold Stadt and the Joseph Stadt nothing in a musical way is produced worth notice, though a capell-meister is there employed to beat the time to songs which are in the regular Astley and Sadler's Wells style. My English proprieties were somewhat scandalized at finding a number of young ladies introduced on the stage here in short tight jackets without tail, silk breeches, and stockings equally tight, a dress calculated to delineate the form with excessive accuracy; and I would leave it to casuists to settle whether the gentleman in black, whom, out of respect and ceremony they will not engage for the Freischütz, would conduce half the mischief to public morals and delicacy by appearing on the stage, that these abandoned and profligate exhibitions do.—In the suburban theatres laughter reigns supreme, and the unities of time, place, &c. are all sacrificed to it; thus, the most sober morning conversation may be interrupted by the entrance of Apollo, or Mercury, or some such unexpected visitor; as for a ghost, it is impossible to know when one may not be expected, and a thing of that sort is as well understood when it comes, and excites no more surprise, than does a banker's clerk in Cheapside at twelve o'clock in the day.

After the theatre, which is soon over, the sound of various bands of music invite the passenger to take his supper in open gardens. No place of refreshment, from the highest to the lowest, is without music; bassoons and clarionets are as " plenty as blackberries," and in the suburbs, at every turn one alights upon fresh carousing, fresh fiddling, fresh illuminations. At night Vienna is in its glory : " What has night to do with sleep ?" is the motto of its inhabitants, and so they prowl about to see fireworks, mountebanks, horsemanship, dancing dogs, &c.; but the Prater is generally the place where attractions of this sort centre. The love of pleasure and of gaiety is the strongest passion in human existence there, but I have not observed the outrageous profligacy by which the city is said to be characterised. Any one who walked without the walls, and saw the myriads of children who play about, might conclude with justice that propagation was at a premium in Vienna. The emperor dearly loves little boys, because they in process of time make tall soldiers, and little girls because they help to multiply the little boys. The boasted cheapness of living there, though true with respect to eating and drinking, does not so clearly manifest itself when the bill for apartments is presented. A person may live at an hotel in Covent Garden for pretty nearly the same money; the master of the inn keeps this formidable item (lodging) in *petto*, which is, compared with the others, as Ossa to a wart, in order that he may soothe the anguish of his guest at departing, a fact which exhibits great tenderness of nature in that personage.

The first *funeral* service that I heard in Vienna took place in St. Stephen's, and consisted of Winter's Requiem in C minor. For this performance the audience were entirely indebted to the benevolence of a foreign ambassador, who most disinterestedly departed this life just at a time when a requiem had become a matter of great rarity. The little organ in the choir, a very sweet-toned instrument, was used with a full orchestra of instruments and voices. The multitude collected round the catafalco, which was blazing with wax-lights, while many beset the choir as though the music promised something great. This cathedral is of all others the place for a solemn dirge, on account of the fine dark hue with which its walls are encrusted, and at this performance it was partly hung with black, and the armorial bearings of the deceased were blazoned throughout it. An immense congregation of priests, divided into two choirs, chaunted the simple Gregorian office for the dead; but the music of Winter, which was afterwards performed, though fine,

struck me as being better adapted for the ordinary
mass than for a requiem. The choruses in it are
masterly, and the flow of harmony quite in the
church style, but it wanted melancholy. I should
not have imagined, in casually hearing the composition, that it was intended to accompany the
last rites of the church over a corpse; the sym-
pathy and interest we all naturally feel on such an
occasion, is best heightened by an extreme simplicity in the music, which quality this wants. Nor
does the admission of stringed instruments at these
times add to the solemnity; the organ and voices
alone are, to my taste, more impressive; but perhaps Mozart's and Cherubini's requiems are those
which must form exceptions to the rule of extreme
plainness. Winter's sweet movement in A flat
was charmingly sung—

After the requiem was finished, a whole procession
of priests and choir paraded the cathedral, at dis-
tant intervals chaunting a Gregorian phrase, accompanied by four trombones, and I have heard
nothing comparable to the delicious effect these instruments produce when heard at a distance in the

cathedral ; their tones are so softened in the space, and they join in the gradual swell of voices upon the silence with a sweet severity. Well might the hearer who had found a seat in the choir remain listening to their echoes as they died away in those arches, and cherishing the expectation of a fresh burst. The faces of the crowd here showed that no *memento mori* could draw them into salutary reflections on the shortness of human life, or the vanity of human wishes; the pace at which the people walked or twirled about upon their heels, had little of the pensive in the action, and showed an utter determination to make the most of the wax candles: but I believe that Death may be found a more entertaining playfellow in a populous city than in a little village ; for if he come as an enemy among a great number, they agree to bully him. The seats in the choir of St. Stephen's are left completely to the public, instead of being occupied, as with us, by singing men ; on the desks are an abundance of fancifully carved animals, in a fine dark wood, given with infinite truth ; horses are lashing out behind, dogs baying the moon, and so forth. They best feel the beauty of the cathedral who take off the hat in it on leaving the street, where the noise and sun's reflexion make silence

and coolness grateful, and, on looking around, the
harmony of colour, the lightness of the architecture, the stained glass, all the foregone grandeur of
taste which has been employed in the construction
of the place, fill the mind with delight.   Here to
speak loud would be to violate the sanctuary; a
spell is upon one's voice as in a gallery of pictures.   The young feet of Haydn as a choir boy,
winding among those pillars, Albrechtsberger too
in the pride of his fugues, and surrounded by a
levee of his pupils, were present to my mind
within this fane.   The absence of all noise is the
next best thing to music.   The Gregorian psalms
were chaunted every day in St. Stephen's, but the
manner of doing it was most slovenly; a *tiny*
voluntary came in upon the organ upon the end of
each psalm, and the organist generally made it
consist of one point of imitation carried through
three or four parts, lasting less than a quarter of a
minute; it was the blossoming of a fugue; the
subject was " no sooner born than blasted."

In this place I have been more than once disgusted at the contrast between the real earnestness
of the poor people at their prayers, many of whom
shrink from observation, and search out the most
retired corners for their devotions, and the open,

unconcealed laughter of the priests at the altar. If these teachers of the ignorant have really a contempt for the ceremonies of their religion, what a shameless fraud are they practising upon the credulity of others.

The people who are authorised to beg in St. Stephen's for the good of the church carry a kind of closed saucepan fixed to the end of a pole, and through a little opening in this machine they implore you to make an *introit* of some part of your personal property. When they wish to stimulate the generosity of donors, which is not unfrequently tardy, they give the saucepan, with all its coppers, a tremendous shake, which action produces a noise as though a sack had been emptied into it. Not being aware of the existence of this ordonnance in the ecclesiastical polity of the Catholics, I was astonished at the enormity of the contributions I heard, and uneasy at not having brought out money enough to keep up with the unobtrusive vastness of donation which resounded on all sides; but at last, behind a pillar, I espied a dignified functionary of the church giving brief and abstracted *whisks* to his copper saucepan. And how did the perfectability of human nature at this sight vanish from my imagination : charity, benevolence, liberality, fled in an instant, and instead of their angel forms there remained only a gentleman flourishing his copper saucepan!—I must record as extremely beautiful the effect of light shed in through stained glass on a little chapel on the right-hand of the great entrance to St. Stephen's—not a ray penetrates but is painted with some rich colour: it is a place for an old silver-haired pope, in gorgeous vestments, to be fancied giving benediction to a kneeling queen; or, as the poet has exquisitely pictured the effect in the girl who has knelt " to ask Heaven's grace and boon,"

> " Rose bloom fell on her hands together prest,
> And on her silver cross soft amethyst,
> And on her hair a glory like a saint."

A Gothic cathedral is to the little children in a city like a venerable kind of elderly acquaintance; many a young Samuel have the inscriptions on its monuments furnished with his earliest lessons in reading; many young limbs has its broad stone floor tempted to a gambol, though it be upon graves: and when the child has grown to a man, and after an absence revisits his old haunts, he finds the cathedral still looks as it did when he was a little boy, nor does it remind him by its altered face that *he* has grown old.

I visited a convent of Franciscan monks—for Vienna boasts "black, white, and grey,"—and conversed with one of that shirtless, dirty, short-cropped and close-shaved community. The cloisters (in the middle of which was a square, dry, and gravelly garden, where a few flowers languished) were ornamented with pictures of the most wretched execution, and equally wretched subjects: here was a carotid artery slit, attended by a very natural gush of blood; there was a head newly divorced from the body, with every particular vessel, nerve, or tegument bare for anatomical inspection: in one place a man was making an involuntary exhibition of his muscle, being flayed alive; in another, a cook, who having scorched himself in roasting, by a natural, though not usual transition, fell into a fit of musing on the intolerable nature of the great fire, commenced saint, and was duly canonized. On all sides might be seen one of the most sanguinary troops in the whole army of martyrs. My ghostly leader observed, that it was fortunate these sacrifices were not called for at the present day; and I gathered from him that Germany would be a bad place to beat up for volunteer recruits to the army of martyrs if the regulars were found inefficient for its service—no commission in it would

have tempted him to enlist. He said Italy had
always produced the most daring heroes that had
ever cut a figure in the profession. The refectory was
so closely swept, and clear of any thing to gratify
carnal appetites, that Lazarillo di Tormes and his
Spanish master might have starved there. The
retirement of a monastery is now the only thing
which will please a traveller in visiting one; the
inmates have not so much of sense in their observations, or disinterestedness in their services, as
they have of a certain strong smell in their persons,
doubtless the odour of sanctity ; and the value of
this must not be under-rated, for there is not a
monk of any standing from whom the " way of the
wind " may not be calculated with the greatest accuracy. In one of the convents in Vienna the
monks are famed for their pianoforte playing, and
give concerts, which are attended by the best artists :
their style of performance has been described to me
by a friend as being very brilliant and ambitious,
but I did not hear it myself.

As Beethoven was, at my visit, no longer to be
found "in the body," I resolved to make a pilgrimage to his tomb ; and the reader will pardon
me for lingering over the grave of this great man
with some of those tender yearnings of spirit which

" Old Mortality " felt for his friends, and which all should feel for those who have given them great pleasure. Beethoven resided in one of a row of tall white houses overlooking the city walls, on the road to Währinge, the prettiest outlet of Vienna. In the cemetery of this quiet little village, in a corner against a low wall, from whence an infinite deal of country may be seen, he reposes, close to the nephew of an English ambassador, who was suddenly killed upon the Prater by falling from his frightened horse. This is the history of his neighbour's end. And here, among rustic chapels, wooden crucifixes, mounds of earth with flowers growing on them— such are the simple memorials—one might become " half in love with easeful death." The place itself might have been, in Beethoven's lifetime, his study, for it was in the green lap of nature and among the old trees that the composer wove his fancies, and not by the flickering of a night-lamp. It is much more pleasant to the imagination that a poet or musician should rest from his labours where the atmosphere is pure above, and where tall plants spring out of the soft earth, than that he should be buried for ever in the cold depths below the pavement of a cloister. A monument is preparing for Beethoven, and a huge unmarked stone covers the

spot of his interment until that shall be ready.
The Germans have a very pretty appellation for
Beethoven ; they call him " Tondichter " (the poet
of sounds), instead of the ordinary name " Ton-
künstler, " (the scientific musician).

How melancholy was the fate of this composer :
condemned, young and ardent, at the age of twenty-
eight, by an incurable deafness, to have his mind
imprisoned for ever within itself, the world of sounds
for ever shut to him, no rural flute, as he himself
pathetically lamented, to disturb in a country walk
the sad monotony of his quiet. Though the poet
is privileged to enjoy, if he please, the morning sun
or the fresh song of the birds without quitting his
apartment, yet confine him to his chamber-thoughts,
and he shall be as miserable as a lover compelled to
live *for ever* on the idea of his mistress. This was
the situation of Beethoven ; yet it must have been
some alleviation to his melancholy that, though unable to share in the pleasure of a new composition,
he could at least read in the smiles on the faces of
his friends a proof of the beauty of his ideas, and
in that version must have enjoyed them.

Beethoven was in youth, like Mozart, a magnificent pianoforte player ; he was not easily coaxed
to sit down to the instrument, or to exert himself,

except for the sake of his own particular intimates;
but when he did so, every one who heard him ac-
knowledged the greatest master of his day. The
difference between the *extemporising* of these two
great men has been thus related to me by a good
judge who had heard both: " Mozart was inspired
in modulation, all the profound and mysterious
affinities of chords were touched upon as his hand
wandered over the keys, there was magic in his
fingers, he had graceful melody and sentiment ever
ready to adorn his subject; but this was mere poetic
luxury to him, he could involve his subject in all
the subtleties of canon, and arrive on the spot at
the result of a mathematical problem. To invent
off-hand in the last-mentioned style is to soar with
weights on the wings. In Beethoven's musical
mind was to be found an undecaying fancy; there
was a tender song in his melodies, great fire and
energy in working up his subject; but the poet
predominated in him too much over the musician
to lead him into the display of that learned and
scholastic treatment of it in which Mozart indulged.
Beethoven was not *integrally* the musician that the
other was, yet in his andantes and other slow movements there is frequently to be found a spirit no less
affectionate and enchanting than Mozart's." In

his younger days Beethoven consented to the juris-
diction of musical laws, and obeyed them; his
earlier pianoforte works, and his first and second
instrumental sinfonias, are pure with respect to
progressions, classical in their episodes and general
construction; but in advanced life he set the pe-
dants too heartily at defiance, as he grew older he
became more tenacious of the merit of those productions in which he had, as it were, trodden on the
confines of forbidden ground, hovering between
genius and extravagance.   When his friends
praised the regularity of his early writings, he
preferred the wildness of his later ones; and there
never yet was, I believe, a writer who did not reserve the weight of his own liking for the sickliest
and ugliest bantlings of his imagination; for what
all the world agrees to call beautiful is in no want
of patronage.

A fac-simile of the card which announced the
order of Beethoven's funeral, to his admirers in
Vienna may not be uninteresting to many in England; for it is a document like this, with its minute
particularity, which, after a few years have elapsed,
recals more forcibly the identity and actual existence of such a man than even his works themselves.

Einladung

zu

Ludwig van Beethoven's

Leichenbegängniss,

welches am 26. März um 3 Uhr Nachmittags Statt finden wird.

Man versammelt sich in der Wohnung des Verstorbenen im Schwarzspanier-Hause Nr. 200, am Glacis vor dem Schottenthore.

Der Zug begibt sich von da nach der Dreyfaltigkeits-Kirche bey den P. P. Minoriten in der Alstergasse.

———————

Die musikalische Welt erlitt denn unersetzlichen Verlust des berühmten Tondichters am 26. März 1827 Abends gegen 6 Uhr. Beethoven starb an den Folgen der Wassersucht, im 56. Jahre seines Alters, nach empfangenen heil. Sacramenten.

Der Tag der Exequien wird nachträglich bekannt gemacht von

L. van Beethoven's

Verehrern und Freunden.

(*Translation of the preceding Card.*)

INVITATION TO LEWIS VAN BEETHOVEN'S FUNERAL,

Which will take place March 29, at Three o'Clock
in the Afternoon.

The Company will assemble in the House of the Deceased,
in the Schwartz Panier House, No. 200, on the Glacis,
before the Scotch Gate. The Procession will go from
thence to the Trinity's Church at the P. P. Minorites, in
the Alser Street.

The Musical World experienced the irreparable loss of
this celebrated Composer on the 26th of March, 1827,
at Six o'Clock in the Evening. Beethoven died of Dropsy,
in the 56th Year of his Age, after having received the
holy Sacraments.

The Day of the Exequies will be made known hereafter,
by L. van Beethoven's Admirers and Friends.

On a visit to Schönbrun I found that a land
storm in the neighbourhood of Vienna is *unique*
in its display of the effect of wind upon dust, and
he who has only encountered a March gale on a
high road in England, knows but little what those
unfortunate Austrians endure, who leave the walls
of their city in dry and dusty weather. The effect
of the visitations is curious; through the closed
windows of the carriage one may be admiring the
sparkling sunshiny morning, the gaiety of the
equipages on the road, the buildings in the distance, but in an instant, by one rending blast, the

roads are swept clean of every atom which a square
foot of dust to every foot of road may contain; the
day's work of thousands of scavengers is done at a
blow; the whole is upwhirled; a solid, dun-coloured
mass rises against the windows, and gives the idea
of solitary imprisonment, or of being buried alive.
With inflamed and tearful eyes I here confess the
value of our own dear, much-undervalued London
mud, and make atonement to that wronged material
for mentally depreciating the gravity and consistency of its character.

The palace of Schönbrun would disappoint those
who like myself had formed to themselves the
imagination of a princely building, sheltered by
and embosomed in lofty trees. The thought of a
summer residence suggests such a fancy, but the
building has nothing of the sort; the front of it is
like the palace at Versailles, open to the road, and
behind are the gardens, the only ones I have seen
in Germany laid out in the French taste, with
trees cut into walls, fountains with river-gods, &c.;
some piece of exquisite formality to arrest the attention of the visitor at every step. The palace itself,
in the time of Maria Theresa the scene of infinite
revelry and feasting, is now deserted, and among
whole suites of magnificent apartments there is

nothing but the walls left to admire. Here and
there may be indeed found a common bedstead, a
few chairs, such miserable chamber apparatus as
might be brought in to make two or three rooms
tenantable after a general seizure of furniture had
taken place. The mother of the young Napoleon
occasionally sleeps in the palace when she visits
her son, who, with his tutors, inhabits a wing of
the building. By a particular grace of the guide,
who is here of a very trusting disposition, a
stranger may be as excursive as he pleases, pass
from room to room alone without listening to
tedious explanations, until he almost fancies himself wandering in that noiseless palace of the
Arabian tales, where by degrees the voice of a
young man reading the Koran aloud interrupts the
silence. There are no pictures except a few portraits, and a representation of the dinner and supper at the espousals of Joseph II.; the figures in
the last two pictures are multitudinous, and are
very carefully finished; but the freshness with
which the paintings have lasted, and will still last,
appears to satirize the brief grandeur of the events
they commemorate, to make one think how short-
lived are the proud moments of kings, even when
they are most " valiant to eat and to drink, to

mingle their wines, and to throw the rest upon the stones." The young Napoleon frequents the opera-house in Vienna; I have seen him there, but his face does not appear very intelligent; he may sometimes be found in the grounds. The palace and gardens of Schönbrun are now a splendid soli-tude; in an hour's ramble I met only a student strolling along the broad garden walks, with a book for his companion. Here are also to be seen a melancholy, half-civilized old lion, a pensive elephant, and a bear or so, whose little intercourse with mankind renders them surly and unattractive after the elegant society and agreeable hyenas of Exeter 'Change.

When the English are out on a travelling expe-dition, their insatiable curiosity to see strange cities, and their contempt of distance and fatigue for its gratification, is so perfect, that they astonish foreigners, and perplex their more sober country-men. Let the phrenologists settle the organ which prompts an Englishman in Vienna to take a *run* to Constantinople, without any other object than to gaze about him; this was an excursion that was seriously propounded to me by one who did not know that I had authority to inspect the cymbals, the drums, tambourines, and triangles in that capital.

The sensation produced by being in a new city soon wears itself out by repetition; but the constant variety in the manners and disposition of a people does not so soon tire the observer. There is a cockneyism in the Viennese dialect, which the very people who use, go and laugh at in the imitation of a man at the Joseph Stadt Theatre. In this broad caricature every one of the audience is content to enjoy the joke at his neighbour's vulgarity, but it is done very good-naturedly. The inhabitants of Berlin and Vienna turn each other into ridicule on the stage most heartily and unreservedly. If you purchase any article of a poor person in Vienna, the acknowledgment of your bounty is always " Küss die hand " (I kiss your hand), and the word is generally followed by the deed.

The ladies in Vienna have remarkably delicate complexions, fine hair, and pretty features; they dress very gaily in the Parisian fashion, and have an extreme consciousness of their appearance in this respect; but from my own observation, and it was a careful one, I should think it a rare thing to find in Vienna a female face with that *inward* look of sentiment, tenderness, and intellect, for which a man might with perfect propriety become madly in love. That I should rob them of a grace, Heaven forfend; they have in conversation the elegant languor and fashionable *nonchalance* which are highly esteemed as feminine accomplishments, but the fascination of the Saxon women will not allow me to speak even of these impartially.

The flippancy of taste displayed by the more fashionable concert-goers in Vienna may be imagined from an exhibition of instrumental playing with which they were entertained on one occasion when I was present, the prominent parts of which were variations for the violin, performed by Madame Parravacini, and the first movement of Hummel's pianoforte concerto in B minor played by Frederic Wörlitzer, of Berlin, a boy thirteen years old. The lady's violin performance required much politeness and self-command to restrain laughter, it was so extremely bad, and particularly in some rapid *staccato* passages near the bridge, where the defiance of tune was droll; the boy, though well tutored, got through his task without conveying the slightest pleasure. Both these performers seemed to attract in proportion as the individuals were unfit to manage their instruments— the lady to *fiddle*, or the boy to play on the pianoforte. We have had so much of child's play lately in England, that it is to be hoped the fashion is on the decline; for if extremes be good, how much better would it be to employ those " whose tops are bald with dry antiquity," and to let the superannuated have a chance; because, if we did not there get rapidity we might get sentiment, which is a better thing. Common listeners frequently imagine, that provided the mere notes are played, the end of music is accomplished, forgetting that the mind of the performer should show itself in the light in which he understands a passage, and then, instead of being a mere automaton, with a number of ready-made graces bestowed upon his mechanism, we should have the emanation of his feeling and sensibility struck out in a momentary impulse. Too many lads have been made players and singers because they have elastic fingers or loud voices, who are wholly destitute of the musical gift perhaps even of ear. If physical advantages as well as genius be necessary to make a player, it is a pity wholly to discard the latter ingredient, and to let the former shift for itself. Weber's overture to Euryanthe was not so well played as at Darmstadt; the opera orchestra in Vienna has correctness, but less of tone than others of Germany. The last piece of this concert was a *scena,* the composition of Cadolini; it was accompanied by a chorus, and intended to display the powers of Mademoiselle Lalande to advantage. I had hoped to leave Vienna with a pleasurable recollection of this lady, who really *can* sing well, but my chronicle would not be faithful if I were not to say that the affair was most silly and frivolous. About twenty men in black came streaming in with much solemnity as a chorus, but more for the purpose of making a half circle round Madame Lalande, who stood radiant in smiles and whiteness, the centre of attraction, and screamed one of the vilest compositions I ever heard. The audience of the opera at Vienna, with its worthless overheaped applause, its *bravoes* ever bestowed in the wrong place, would destroy the modesty and discretion of the best singer that ever appeared on this earth. The Viennese are for their pains heartily welcome to the enjoyment of those whom they have thus schooled; Lablache is the only actor and singer of whom I would rob them: but to those in England who expect discrimination and judgment in a metropolitan audience, I would say, seek it rather among Austrian boors.

Canova's tomb to Christina, queen of Sweden, in the church of the Augustines, is one of the prettiest designs which I have ever seen on a monument; the stepping grace of the figures, who form a funeral procession, is admirable. The last grand mass of Cherubini in D was performed here, but I was driven from the church by the vile organ-playing, the effect of which may only be compared to the noise a drowning man might be supposed to make every time his head emerged from the water. In this church are to be seen, partly clad in finely laced and bespangled clothes, the skeletons of St. Vincent and St. —— lying on their sides in glass coffins, grinning and showing their teeth and breast bones, noseless and eyeless, to scare little children.

The most favourite subjects of the painters for ornamenting Catholic churches are decidedly the assumption of the Virgin and the last judgment: in the first, the Madonna floating in ether, and surrounded by her winged guard of light infantry, there is nothing but what is pretty and appropriate; but in the second, some of the angels are erroneously represented with their pikes, taking an ungenerous advantage of the inverted position in which several misguided individuals are, from a considerable height, " with hideous ruin and combustion," hurrying down to the abyss. It would appear a sort of wantonness ill consistent with the angelic character, not to soothe any one in that melancholy situation; as if to have the heels in the air upon so long a journey, with no chance of *righting*, were not enough without adding another sting to the reflections on the way: the painters must have grossly misconceived their subject.

The church music performed at the Imperial Chapel, under the direction of Eybler, is the most delicate and finished service to be heard in Vienna. Sinfonias and full instrumental pieces are sometimes executed there in those parts of the service in which a voluntary on the organ is used among us. Eybler produces a new mass or motett for every great event publicly celebrated by the court; but I do not very much admire the style of this master, his musical thinking is not sufficiently independent; in many compositions that I have heard, he introduces too frequently old phrases of melody, which, however good in Haydn's time, are now worn out.

J. R. von Seyfried, of Vienna, is one of the best living writers for the church now in Germany; there is great fancy in the design, and abundant skill in the construction of his pieces. I heard a motett in B flat, *Dextera Domine*, composed by Seyfried for a soprano *concertante* and a full choir, performed by a musical society in Vienna; although the model of this movement was clearly borrowed from the theatre, it is vain to declaim against the innovation now that the practice is sanctioned by constant imitation. As a piece of writing, there was much to admire in the combination of the orchestra, and the disposal of the accompaniment. Seyfried also adapted with infinite judgment and good taste the musical part of the service which accompanied Beethoven's funeral procession to instrumental movements of the deceased composer. These movements were arranged for four voices (two tenors and two basses) and four trombones; one of them was part of the celebrated *Marcia Funebre*, in an old pianoforte sonata, the others were manuscript scraps which were never incorporated by Beethoven into any great work, though they would have adorned one. There are some extraordinary originality and boldness of harmony in the *Amplius.**

---

* ACCOUNT OF THE FUNERAL OF BEETHOVEN, AND HISTORY OF THE ACCOMPANYING COMPOSITIONS.

As the friends and admirers of Beethoven had, by a large distribution of invitation cards, been made generally acquainted that his solemn public interment would take place on the afternoon of March 3, 1827, a vast multitude, spectators as well as mourners, collected in and before the dwell-

One of the most useful labours of Seyfried is shown in his revision and editorship of the whole

ing of the deceased, Schwartzpanier Haus, on the glacis by the Scotch Gate.

At three o'clock the corpse was brought out—eight singers of the Opera-house, Eichberger, Schuster, Cramolini, A. Müller, Hoffmann, Rupprecht, Borschitzky, and A. Wranitzky, having offered to carry it on their shoulders. After the priest had pronounced a few prayers, the singers performed a grave chorale of B. A. Weber, and the whole procession moved forwards in the following order :

1. The cross-bearer. 2. Four trombone players—the brothers Böck, Waidl, and Tuschky. 3. The master of the choir, M. Assmayer, and under his direction, 4. A choir of singers—M. Tietze, Schnitzer, Gross, Sikora, Frühwald, Geissler, Rathmeyer, Kokrement, Fuchs, Nejebse, Ziegler, Perschl, Leidl, Weinkopf, Pfeiffer, and Seipelt, which, alternately with the trombone quartett, performed the Miserere. This walking orchestra was immediately followed by, 5. The high-priest. 6. The coffin, borne by the abovementioned opera-singers, and attended by the chapel-masters Eybler, Hummel, Seyfried, and Kreutzer on the right, and Weigl, Gyrowetz, Gänsbacher, and Würfel upon the left, as pall-bearers. On both sides, from the beginning of the procession to the coffin, were the torch-bearers, thirty-six in number, consisting of poets, authors, composers, and musicians, among whom were M. Anschütz, Bernard, Böhm, Castelli, Carl Czerny, Signor David, Grillparzer, &c. &c. the whole in full mourning, with white roses and bunches of lilies fastened to the crape on their arms. Next followed Beethoven's brother (the last friend of his youth and his executor), the pupils of the Conservatorio, and the scholars

theoretical works of Albrechtsberger, which performances are received in Germany as the most

of capell-meister Drechsler, the thorough bass teacher of
St. Ann's, the whole deeply lamenting the loss which music
had sustained.

In the church, during the blessing, the choir sang the
" Libera me, Domine, de morte æterna," originally composed by Seyfried with orchestral accompaniments for use
at the performances of Mozart's Requiem, now, however,
arranged merely as a vocal chorus. The corpse was from
hence carried in a hearse to the cemetery at Währinge, followed by many carriages.

At the cemetery M. Anschütz, the actor, surrounded by
a circle of mourners, recited a discourse to the memory of
the departed, written by Grillparzer. Baron von Schlecta
and M. Castelli read short but eloquent poems to the sor-
rowing multitude; and before the grave was closed M. Haslinger put into the hands of Hummel, who was standing
near him, three wreaths of laurel, which were sunk upon
the coffin. The mourners waited until the earth was
smoothed over Beethoven.

The history of the Miserere performed is as follows:
When Beethoven was, in the autumn of the year 1812,
visiting his brother, at that time an apothecary in Lintz, he
was requested by the cathedral chapel-master of that place,
M. Glöggl, to compose for him an *equale* for four trombones,
as such is usually performed on the festival of All Souls.
Beethoven willingly undertook the task, and put together
two very short but masterly compositions. This valuable
MS. having fallen into the hands of M. Haslinger of
Vienna, he, on the morning of the 26th of March, 1827,
when all hope of Beethoven's recovery had been given over,

enlarged and scientific disquisitions into the science
that have appeared, the author having not only the
mind of a practical and experienced musician, but
also the power of communicating clearly and phi-
losophically the principles upon which he combined
and wrote. A great composer is certainly not
obliged to take his thoughts to pieces and reduce
them to their elements, not to look at the roots of
all his harmonies to see whether he has made false
resolutions or not ; he *feels* their effect to be good :
but the greater number of musicians, who have not
so infallible a gift of genius, find study and reflection the next best guides to correctness in composition. It is seldom, if ever, that the poorest compositions that appear in Germany are ungramma-
tical or erroneous in counterpoint ; and this may be
attributed partly to the aristocracy of science there,
which shames pretenders, and partly to the great
quantity of treatises, in which there is scarcely a
questionable point in the art left undiscussed, so
that every one who will write may inform himself

repaired with it to capell-meister Seyfried, with a request
that he would adapt the words of the Miserere to this
equale, that the body of the prince of musicians might be
accompanied to its everlasting rest by its own creations.
M. Seyfried, in pursuance of this idea, undertook the work,
which was finished the night following Beethoven's death.

MISERERE.

AMPLIUS.

previously.—Almost all the composers now residing
in Vienna keep music-shops: Czerny, Diabelli,
Weigl, &c. each has his own bank for the coinage
of his brain; and instead of trafficking, as Haydn
and Mozart did, with music-sellers, they think
that having skill to invent music, they may have
wisdom enough to sell it, a mode of reasoning
which cannot have its propriety impugned by those
who think an author entitled to as much money as
his work will fetch.

Every music lover who visits Vienna will like to
know that Mozart lived in the Rauhenstein Gasse,
a narrow street leading down to the cathedral, in a
house now a tavern or drinking-house, which, by
some remarkable coincidence, wears on its front a
badge of fiddles and other musical instruments.
No one must be so deluded as to imagine, that
when Mozart arrived at his own home he knocked
at a street door as ordinary mortals do; no, he
walked under a gateway, and thence up stairs to
his ordinary apartments. That Mozart gave his
Sunday evening concerts, and enchanted people in
a room on the first floor with a bow window to it,
is a fact not to be despised, for if we fancy the
human being, we must give him a local habitation,
else he is a spirit, and not one of ourselves.

We do not wish to know the great performances of great men, we wish to know their *little* actions, how they walked, looked, and spoke, their crooked habits and peculiarities; and to know that Mozart had a restless and nervous fidgetiness in his hands and feet, and seldom sat without some motion of them, makes him more present to us than the most laboured picture. And here lived Mozart; he who has thrown a fresh grace around the ideal of womanliness, who *could* " paint the rose and add perfume to the violet;" and in love, while the subtle and metaphysical poets are trying to get at the heart of its emotions, gives us straight a language for sighs and tears, for tenderness and rapture. The difference between Mozart and other great composers, such as Haydn for instance, is, that while the latter economize their subjects, he could ever trust to the wealth of his feelings, he saved nothing on paper; he took rural excursions, not to look for thoughts but to enjoy sensation, and began to write when the throng of ideas became insupportable to him. Music was with him, as a certain poet said of verses, a secretion. There is one melancholy of the style of Gluck, and another melancholy of Mozart; that of the first seems like the despondency of a lover who parts with his mistress for ever, the other has more of the caressing pensiveness which one may imagine in a being who enjoyed in a summer arbour by moonlight the song of nightingales, with his head all the time resting in the lap of his mistress. What an enviable perfection must have been Constance Weber's in filling such a mind as Mozart's with beautiful images, in suggesting such an air as " Porgi Amor," or in creating the bitter sweet regrets of " Dove sono." Almost the whole of the songs in Mozart's operas are a continuation of the same spirit which made him in infancy ask his friends, " Do you love me ?" and they show that he who asked for affection could return it with interest. As the excess of the passion in a man of genius ever helps him in the completion of the greatest designs, let it be to the praise of women, that besides that one element in which he reigned supreme, Mozart was of all musicians at once the best lover, and the most refined, various, and intellectual composer that the world has produced.

PRAGUE.

THE situation which this city maintained fifty years since in the superiority of its musical taste over the rest of Germany, is now usurped by Berlin; not that the Bohemians love the art less than formerly, or that they have imbibed the flippant, common-place notions of musical beauty which prevail in Vienna, but that their city is gone out of fashion, and it resigns its dictatorship and arbitration on musical points, to places in which there is more of the thronging and bustling of the world. Mozart would not trust his Clemenza di Tito and Don Juan to make their appearance in Vienna, but despatched them to Prague; in our day Weber sent his opera Der Freischütz from Dresden to Berlin, for this last place is one in which a young artist may be sure of having a liberal judgment passed upon his abilities, with the advantage that if he really achieve a good thing his fame spreads more rapidly from this part of Germany than any other.

Prague has an appearance of decayed magnificence; the narrow streets of the old town look somewhat gloomy in the superb architecture of mansions, once the residence of proud Bohemian nobles, but now occupied by Jew bankers and traders; here and there may be seen, cowering over a gateway, with its wide outstretched wings, and vehement head, a huge eagle, or some other work of art, in which the blackness of dirt and neglect cannot obscure the faithfulness and spirit of the execution. Such lofty portals as these, instead of leading into a festive hall, among knights, minstrels, and dames, conduct one into the society of bales of goods, warehousemen, and money-changers, which are a sad sort of antitheses to one another.

There are six-and-thirty churches here, and but one good inn, though that one is of the best, and produces a sort of beer, which to drink iced in the summer-time might make the gods themselves turn pale with envy.

A musician who lives in Prague with an unmixed devoted attachment to his art, will find no ostentation or pretence in the habits of the professors there ; he will enjoy music in pleasant and easy quarters, with all kinds of town and country beauties, gardens, views, and grand buildings for his walks and recreation, among a simple and good-hearted people, who live to themselves for enjoyment and happiness, without the drudgery of a too active business. There is a calm enthusiasm in all the Bohemians do; they acquire for the most part a greater skill in instrumental music than any other class of Germans, from their firmness of purpose and desire for the best. Where people live out of the great world as they do here, with a common interest in one pursuit, in a picturesque and romantic country, with money sufficient to procure those luxuries which are necessary to imaginative and enjoying persons, they must be amiable; Nature herself looks amiable, which is more than one may say every day of the week in Holland. Life affords few pleasures greater than the view, on a clear and genial day, from the bridge over the Moldau; looking over that wide, calm, and shallow river, to the green islands with which it is spotted, the right bank, which rises into a sudden elevation, is covered with a thick shaggy verdure of short trees and shrubs; in a line with the bridge, and on a level with the height I have mentioned, stand the cathedral and the king's palace, half hidden from view by some stately churches. On Sundays, the visitors of the cathedral, after toiling up the

weary and steep ascent to it, stand for a few minutes to take breath, and gaze round them at the
beautiful panorama of the city and its environs.
Some of the younger people prefer, instead of
hearing a mass, to stroll into the woods close by,
and enjoy the same view in a more perfect solitude.
Various summer-houses in this neighbourhood are
haunted by parties from the city, who repair hither
with their wine, their provisions, and their pipes,
for an afternoon's sociality.   As ladies in Germany
do not object to tobacco-smoke, they are not prevented by the last-mentioned item from contributing
to the pleasure of the entertainment.

The islands on the Moldau are sacred to pleasure ; on that one denominated the Greater Venice,
there are frequent rifle-matches, and some of the
marksmen of the Freischütz Society here have balls
as true as though the black huntsman himself had
forged them.   In the evening there is always
dance-music or concert-music, and the raft, which
is ever pushing from the shore to the island, and
back again, is never without its full complement of
listeners or performers. On one occasion, in waiting
at the extremity of this pretty and verdant nest,
thinking of my passage homewards, I was induced
to remain by an unexpected but very agreeable

concert: after sunset, and on a fine calm river, very poor music will generally please; but to stand where the soft turf under one's feet slopes gently down into the water, and to hear from a raft as it paddles about on a broad and quiet stream, about twenty men's voices joined in a solemn madrigal, is a rare delight. This was mine; the performers glided by slowly in the cool and refreshing air of the river; the stars were above their heads, there was repose and silence in the whole scene around them; they stood up singing by heart; and it appeared to me the highest luxury imaginable thus to pour out tones spontaneously, making a rich and mellow harmony, without the trouble of *thinking* of parts, and giving up their souls as it were to the influence of quietness and the beautiful shadows around them. The birds do this; they seem inspired when they have found out some " melodious plot, of beechen green;" and the Germans imitate them, inasmuch as they prefer having their music to flow from them with as little necessity as possible for reading it, thus devoting themselves entirely to its expression and character.

Although half the cathedral of Prague has been destroyed by fire in the *religious* (or religion's) wars, as they are called in Germany, what remains of it has more antique curiosities, and more costly and regal ornaments than I have yet seen. The casque of its knightly founder is shown with great reverence, and the more so as the skull which it contained was battered to atoms, and the brains dashed against the altar by his loving brother. The naked roofless walls, the isolated remnants of pillars through which the passage to the serviceable part of the edifice is found, show it to have been the seat of great priestly magnificence, and there is here still a whole sacred composition, consisting of groups of figures as large as life, wrought in solid silver, which has somehow or other escaped that levy on church valuables which the wars have rendered expedient. The pictures here are principally by Hans Holbein, and Albert Durer. Old Bohemian barons lie in separate chapels, stark on their backs; with some of them the noses are dismally mutilated : no heroes were better than these, romances assure us, in withstanding the suffocating stench and poison spume of enchanted dragons, or in some dismal valley, of supporting themselves when pecked at, for a fortnight together, by the most fiery and exasperated of drakes. The sacristan of this cathedral, who undertook to explain to us the mysteries of the place, as well as a jargon

of bad French, bad German, bad Latin, and good
Bohemian, would allow us to understand, seemed
aboriginal ; he appeared never to have been out of
those aisles, or to know more of the world than a
man learns by pointing out tombs and living among
the dead. His conversation, out of habits of deference and respect, was accompanied by such
strange and inexplicable noises in his throat, such
a *girning* and grinding in that quarter, that if we
had not been assured he was a tame sacristan, we
might have imagined a wild beast in our company.
The great organ here is so large that it is only
used for two great festivals of the year, which is no
very wise plan for improving the tone of it, or
keeping its intonation exact ; the rats, who have
made their habitations in the great pipes, may look
upon these times as their equinoctial gales, and
weather them without grumbling. Two small instruments, which are used alternately on common
Sundays, are voiced so extremely loud as to be unpleasant to listen to. The organist Wenzel is a
good player ; and his deputy, who assisted on some
occasions, would have pleased me better had he restrained the velocity of his fingers. There is excellent music in this place, the band is choice, and
there is the sweetest choir of boys' voices that I

have heard out of England. On Sunday afternoon,
as I entered the cathedral doors, the responses of
an imploring Gregorian litany were going forward.
There was such a hearty irresistible earnestness in
one of the *rises* of this fervent old melody, that I
could hardly wonder at the obstreperous devotion
of a man near me, who almost yearned himself into
a fit as he sung it; at every succeeding " *Libera
nos, Domine,*" his transport became more exquisite.
A monk who knelt before him would have made a
picture for Rembrandt; the saint-like calmness of
his face, his rich beard, his loose drapery, his fingers wandering mechanically among his beads;
without singing, or even appearing to pray, he
looked so rapt, his eye so immoveable, that I fancied the presence of one of those holy fathers
whom the painters have represented as ripe for a
celestial vision.

The drivers of the fiacres in Prague are a race
of hackney coachmen that have this notable distinction in their moral constitution—they are
always satisfied with their fares. One of these
people whom I hired, undertook the task of ex-
plaining what was worthy of notice in the churches,
a piece of supererogatory benevolence shown to me
purely out of complaisance as a stranger. I stared

when he made me the proposition, forgetting for the instant that he was not one of those whose consciences are seared and feelings indurated by wet weather and gin drinking. It was not the genius of gruffness, who in England descends from a coach-box in a pair of dank old boots, his hat wreathed with a wisp of straw, in a series of great coats which nourish his discontent without adding to his vivacity. So difficult is it for an English-man to comprehend the actual perfectability of a character, the vices of which are purely local.

The Conservatorio of Prague furnishes Germany, Russia, and France with some of the best of their singers and players, and it is the principal assistance to the cultivation of good music in the city. Every year the numbers of the pupils are thinned—the elder young men are drafted off to different or-chestras, the young women to different operatic establishments. Here Mademoiselle Sontag, whom I have not yet heard, was a pupil. Moscheles is also of Prague. The director of the Conservatorio is M. Weber, a professor well calculated for the task he undertakes; the violin professor is Pixis, brother of the pianoforte player of that name now in Paris, and a real lover of his art. The house in which the exercises are carried forward is a large and handsome building, remote from the street, standing in a garden ornamented with statues : there is a wild unpruned luxuriance about the shrubs, and a dinginess about the figures, that does not look much like diligent gardening, but there is greenness and seclusion and quiet for the young musicians. Here I found groups of young men chatting away their leisure before the commencement of the afternoon's practice : it did not seem to have tinged their countenances or conversation with melancholy, that music and the perfecting of sinfonias was the serious business of their lives. On certain days in the week all individual *blasting* and *bowing* ceases, and the young men play in concert. The composition given this afternoon was Mozart's Jupiter sinfonia, and it was played with a precision and degree of execution that astonished me. The times of the *allegro* and *finale* were taken much faster than is customary with the composition in England, which of course put the readiness of these young people upon their several instruments to the test. Not a point failed, and I could plainly discern that each pupil understood the construction of the whole work in score as well as the execution of his own part, from the propriety with which the various features were given. The fugue in the last movement, of which the points are so close and the motion so contrary, was played with infinite spirit and correctness; and an operatic scena and a full overture closed the performance.

In attending the concerts of a conservatorio, one hears more good playing than good effect, because the parts are not equally balanced; here there was a complete chorus of horns and other wind instruments, which predominated over the stringed band, and made the resonance of the *forte* parts immensely overpowering, though their room was tolerably large.

Another part of the building was furnished with a miniature theatre for the performance of operas; and here Mozart, Cimarosa, Paisiello, and others, offered studies in dramatic singing to the female pupils, and a school of accompaniment to the instrumentalists. In the first act of the " Cosi fan tutti " I found in one of the girls a most charming Dorabella, of a voice and grace of action perfectly exquisite. I cannot but think that an establishment of this sort, where the student enters without the thought of getting money as his primary object, and where he receives his musical education *gratis*, with a mere restriction as to the term of his ap-

prenticeship, is the best nursery for young professors, inclining them to value their art for itself,
and not as a pander to their vanity or avarice.

The interior of the opera-house in Prague is long,
narrow, and dark, except upon the stage : so little
does it appear like a place of gaiety, where the
audience are to divide a satisfaction in looking at
one another, with the business before them, that
they are not supposed to have a thought but for
the piece. The *petit-maître* and coquette in the
boxes may languish or gnash their teeth in outer
darkness. Every thing about this building was
intensely interesting to me from the association it
bore in the mind with the great operas of Mozart,
as there was nothing extraneous to divert; music
might here, in gaining applause, gain it pure and
undivided. The old leather-seated chairs in the
orchestra, the old instrument with its old-fashioned
black keys, which had been used in accompanying
the recitatives of the Don Giovanni, became, when
connected with the memory of Mozart, matters of
dignified conjecture—his presence redeemed the
most trifling object from indifference. In this
quaker-like opera-house all gilding and burnishing
is set at nought; there is an admirable band, and
by some of the elder members of it Mozart is not

yet forgotten. I was pleased to hear of the hurry
with which the overture to the Don Giovanni was
finished, and of the parts being brought out into
the orchestra; to feel myself upon the very spot
of his triumphs, and to shudder in imagination
with the audience when that terrible horseman, " Il
Commendatore," the man of stone, bows his head
to the supper invitation. The primitive simplicity
of manners among the people in the orchestra, to
whose acquaintance I was introduced, gave me
much pleasure; and I won their good-will in three
ways—by being an Englishman, by visiting such
an *auld warld* place as Prague, where any out-
landish European is a phenomenon, and by liking
German music.

In theatrical representations, the Germans are
famous for domestic tragedy; they will sit mutely
absorbed in the most heartbreaking family catastrophe, and take a pleasure in that painful fidelity
of acting, which to my melancholy northern blood
is almost insupportable. During a feast of this
sort the other night, when the whole house was
still as a stone, and all were most luxuriously
desponding, a lady near me, at a critical moment,
gave one loud and solitary sneeze, which was irresistible; the audience simultaneously tittered, but

it put a more cheerful aspect on life, and reconciled us to the vicissitudes of things. Die Schweitzer Familie (the Swiss Family) of Weigl, which was performed here, has for its principal interest the sadness of a home-sick girl, who is distracted between desire to return to her native country, and anxiety for the happiness of a generous lover, whom she fears to leave. It is hard to understand the *maladie du pays*, or to give any sympathy to men or women who live with the object of their idolatry; for to my own thinking, in such a case England, France, or Illyria would be the same. Of the music of this opera it may be said, that there is a want of variety in the sentiment; the songs become tiresome, because the grief of the daughter is like the grief of the father and the grief of the mother and the grief of the lover, " for egad they 're all in a tale;" they whine, and are extremely pitiful and sad; but one feels to resent such behaviour, and wishes them all at the deuce. To reach the grandeur of calamity, that desolation of heart which makes the impassioned Donna Anna the sublimest of Mozart's creations, is to get at the profoundest of dramatic expression, but *puling* is very wide from an heroic melancholy. I did not like the accompaniments to Die Schweitzer Familie; there was an affected plainness about them; the violins, in eternal octaves to the melody, left the orchestra but few effects. At rehearsal in the morning the band played an overture in E by Kreutzer which was worthy a snug hearing; in five minutes it said more for the orchestra than Weigl's music would in as many hours; there was an uproar of applause at its close, the author had thrown into his composition so many racy passages. Inventions of this sort, though caviare to the musical multitude in England, are readily detected in Bohemia; and the *nonsense* of instrumental music, such as unmelodious or inconsequent phrases, and the injudicious conduct of a piece, or an unlucky modulation, have little chance of passing muster. There was plenty of amusement at rehearsal, for the music-director and some women who were trying over songs for a new opera, seasoned their morning's work with a world of pleasantries.—The present maestro is a little wizened old man, remarkable for the quaint singularity of his dress, and his long hair, parted and streaming over his shoulders. Having found that his compositions will not do for the people of Prague, he ensconceth himself in his strong-hold as singing-master, in which capacity he is really excellent.

With a counterfeit surliness in his voice and look,
he sometimes sits in the orchestra eyeing a poor
girl on the stage, and as she sings doubtingly,
points to some particular inch of the throat from
which the sound proceeds; but he does not quit
his remarks nor renewed beginnings until the tone
comes forth from the proper quarter.—C. M. von
Weber was formerly director of the opera in
Prague, but quitted the place on his marriage, to
reside at Dresden. At the time of his employment
here, he had composed no work of importance,
merely cantatas and songs, with full accompaniments; and the good fortune of this musician is
worthy observation, as a circumstance I believe
altogether unprecedented in the history of the art.
That a man should live on to within a few years of
forty in obscurity, not distinguished in Germany
from a host of the same stamp; that he should be
as little endowed by nature as any composer that
ever lived with a store of melody such as the popu-
lace might troll about to gladden themselves; yet
by one work just suited to the cast of his genius,
to leap at once into the most extraordinary favour
throughout Europe, not only gaining credit for
that he had done, but a certain passport for what
he might do; to be invited to foreign countries,

wreathed with laurel in concert-rooms, deafened with applause, and made a show of every where, is a wonderful concatenation of events in the life of a middle-aged gentleman.

The dinners at the Schwartzen Ross in Prague were exemplary, but what pleased me best was the extreme gaiety of the company; the animal spirits of the people were always up at one height, not-withstanding the enormously heavy duty they laid upon their gastric juices. The good-fellowship which reigned here certainly helped the digestive process. In England we constantly meet the same round of faces at our dinner-tables, and should any thing run cross in our affairs, each is ready with its sym-pathy; but here if one is inclined to be miserable and bilious, to hear two or three yards off the most vigorous and rib-moving roars of laughter, nothing can be more effective in leading to a philosophical reflection on the impropriety of indulging meagrims.

The Germans are extremely early risers, and are stirring soon after three o'clock in the summer-time, to enjoy their mineral water-drinkings, public breakfasts, &c.; and they are helped in their ex-traordinary diligence by the ingenious uncomfort-ableness of their beds, which certainly furnish no temptation to sloth, being so extremely short, and with such an accumulation of pillow, that it is no unusual thing to find on waking, the head deposited in the middle of the bed, with the legs, heaven knows! incumbent upon the air. Mr. Coleridge seems to have felt the inconvenience of the chamber apparatus in Germany; for, upon some part of their bed-furniture he says, than use it " I would rather travel like a wild Indian with a blanket round me."

One benefit of the cheapness of learning here is, that a gentility of mind is begotten among a class of human beings who, from their station in life, if left without the knowledge of any thing beyond their handicraft, must inevitably have become the saddest vulgarians. The poorest gipsy-looking youth, who as a mechanic tramps about the country looking for employment, can talk sensibly of books or music; he knows the lives of celebrated men, and the affairs of his country: as for modesty of deportment and civility in his intercourse with strangers, they are never separate from him. A lady at Vienna, who had possessed me on a short acquaintance with the idea that she was an enthusiastic amateur of music, from the volubility with which she ran over the names of composers and compositions, staggered my good opinion of her knowledge by being considerably affected at finding that Handel was dead. No poor itinerant mechanic of the country, I will venture to say, believes Handel (bodily) to be a living composer; and the anecdote serves as a commentary upon the superficiality which passes current in polite conversation for knowledge, and which is put on pretty much to the same end as fine dress.

Mozart's first mass in C was attempted in St. Jacob's church of this city—to say *executed*, unless in the sense of *murdered*, would be improper. This was my crowning experience of the music in a conventual church, which should be ever shunned by those who would preserve their ears from martyrdom, as the monks give a free indulgence to their band to be as out of tune as they please. As I was in the heart of the church, and unwilling to disturb the multitude at prayers, I sat shrinking with horror in the anticipation of those passages where I knew the performers would fail more particularly—the *Credo* and *Et incarnatus est*, with the bustling accompaniments of the first movement, and the difficult time of the second, were full of discordancy and confusion.

I received some reparation for the disappointment of this Sunday morning's service by attending at

St. Michael's the performance of a requiem by Tomaschek, who is the principal composer now residing in Prague. This composition (in C minor) is so well divested of all *Mozartean* reminiscences, so sound in its construction and rich in accompaniment, that it takes the highest rank in modern church music. At a concert in the evening I heard from the same composer some canzonets to the poetry of lyrical pieces by Goethe, which showed much feeling and genius in the musician. The name of Tomaschek has only travelled to England by accident, though it is one that should have made its way there on the strength of the admirable works of art with which it is connected.

A few miles from Prague, on the road to Dresden, I passed in the dusk of evening a lonely greystone building, standing among trees and mountains in a most romantic solitude : in this gloomy seclusion some young girls have chosen to immolate all worldly hope and joy. The rules of the convent are very severe ; and the talk was in Prague of a young lady who had entered it a short time before, after endowing the community with a fortune of twenty thousand crowns. This is the sad remedy for disappointment in love—to overcome one painful feeling by acquiring another. The value of

the sacrifice is enhanced when it is recollected that
to give up the gaiety of society in Germany, the
tedium vitæ must be great indeed.—In this neighbourhood is the estate of Madame Lacker, who is
said to have acquired a large fortune in England as
a teacher of the pianoforte. I have never heard of
the lady as a musician, but I can answer for her
taste in houses of retirement. In a spot

> " More secret and sequester'd, though but feign'd,
>   Pan or Sylvanus never slept."

When Mozart visited Prague, he resided in a
castle in the beautiful environs of the city, and
there completed some of his most excellent sinfonias and quintetts, as well as opera music.

DRESDEN.

The picturesque charms of Dresden have been so frequently expatiated upon, that it is unnecessary to say more upon them: every one knows that it possesses wide streets, elegant buildings, and good store of pretty girls. In this city may be found a more polished society, a greater attention to the established formalities and etiquette of genteel intercourse, than in other cities of Germany; but unfortunately neither Gothic cathedrals nor strange sacristans to delight—Gothic barbarism is not only banished from the conversation in drawing-rooms, but from the church architecture.

The three principal churches, the Catholic church, the Lady's church, and the Royal Lutheran church, are all enriched with organs * by

* I have preserved an inventory of the stops in the magnificent organs at Dresden, not so much for any actual information it may convey to the musical reader, unless he be acquainted with the mechanism employed in the construction of these instruments, as that in glancing over the list of contents he may please his imagination by fancying with

Silbermann, one of the most renowned builders of
Germany, and whose name (Silverman) very well

what effect a piece of florid and artful counterpoint comes
out of a German organ, where the player sits with a flood of
sound ready to the touch of his fingers, and store of thunder lying harmless at his feet. The thickness, depth, and
independence of the pedals, here vindicate supremely the
poetical ascendancy of the fugue over every other class of
musical composition; and in slow subjects, when the bass
rolls in its ponderousness—there is no disputing it—it is
like the *fiat* of the Omnipotent. As a matter of science it
is worthy consideration how far the structure of our organs
might be improved by uniting the sweet *cathedral* quality of
tone for which those of the Temple, Westminster Abbey, &c.
are noted, with the magnificence of Silbermann. If there
lived now in England a mechanic capable of associating the
best points of the two, a perfect specimen of the kind would
be the result.

CONTENTS OF THE ORGANS IN DRESDEN BUILT BY GOTTFRIED SILBERMANN.

THE ORGAN IN THE ROYAL CHURCH OF THE EVANGELISTS
Has 32 Stops, two Rows of Keys, and Pedals.

OBERWERK.	HAUPTWERK.	PEDAL.
1. Principal .... 8 feet	1. Principal .. 8 feet	1. Trompete .... 8 feet
2. Quintatön .... 16 -	2. Spitzflöte .. 8 -	2. Pausan .... 16 -
3. Gedakt ...... 8 -	3. Bordun .... 16 -	3. Violone .... 8 -
4. Octave ...... 4 -	4. Rohrflöte .. 8 -	4. Sub Bass ...... 16 -
5. Quintatön .... 8 -	5. Cornett .... 4 ranks	5. Principal Bass. 16 -
6. Rohrflöte .... 4 -	6. Octave .... 8 feet	
7. Nassat ...... 3 -	7. Gemshorn .. 4 -	
8. Octave ...... 2 -	8. Quinte .... 3 -	
9. Quinte ...... 1½ -	9. Octave .... 2 -	
10. Siflöte ...... 1 -	10. Tertia ..... 2 -	
11. Mixtur ...... 3 ranks	11. Mixtur .... 4 ranks	
12. Vox humana . 8 feet	12. Cymbel .... 3 -	
13. Undamaris .. 8 -	13. Trompete .. 8 feet	
goes from G.	14. Clarion .... 4 -	
14. Schwebung.		

Besides Stops are Schwebung, Klingel, and Bass-Ventil.
This organ was finished and erected in the year 1720.

describes the quality of their tone.—The Catholic church (having on the outside more the appearance of a Grecian temple) is a beautiful building; the interior takes the eye by storm—dark mahogany, polished and variegated marble, pictures, gold and silver on the altar and organ, make up the colours. The effect of an excellent orchestra is heightened by the structure of this edifice, which admits of a fine echo and reverberation, and the deep bass pipes

THE ORGAN IN THE CHURCH OF OUR LADY

Has three Rows of Keys, Pedals, and 43 Stops.

HAUPT MANUAL.	OBERWERK.	BRUSTWERK.
1. Principal .... 16 feet	1. Principal .. 8 feet	1. Principal .... 4 feet
2. Octave ...... 8 -	2. Quintaden.. 16 -	2. Gedakt ...... 8 -
3. Cornett ...... 5 ranks	3. Gedakt .... 8 -	3. Rohrflöte .... 4 -
4. Viola di Gamba 8 feet	4. Octava .... 4 -	4. Nassat ...... 3 -
5. Octave ...... 4 -	5. Quintatön . 8 -	5. Octava ...... 2 -
6. Rohrflöte .... 8 -	6. Rohrflöte .. 4 -	6. Gemshorn ... 2 -
7. Spitzflöte .... 4 -	7. Nassat .... 3 -	7. Quinta ...... 1½ -
8. Quinta ...... 3 -	8. Octava .... 2 -	8. Sifflöte ...... 1 -
9. Octava ...... 2 -	9. Tertia .... 2 -	9. Mixtur ...... 3 ranks
10. Tertia .... 2 -	10. Mixtur .... 4 ranks	10. Chalmeaux .. 8 feet
11. Mixtur ...... 4 ranks	11. Vox humana 8 feet	
12. Cymbel ...... 3 -		
13. Fagott........ 16 feet		
14. Trompete .... 8 -		

PEDAL.

1. Untersatz .... 32 feet.	Wood.
2. Principal Bass .... 16 -	-
3. Pausan........................ 16 -	Metal.
4. Octave Bass .... 8 -	
5. Octave .... 4 -	
6. Mixtur .... 6 ranks	
7. Trompete.................... 8 feet	
8. Clarin Bass .... 4 -	

Besides Stops there are Tremulant, Schwebung, Bass-Ventil (Coppel), and Klingel.

This instrument was completed in the year 1736.

of Silbermann's organ roll their heavy notes into the square, arresting every passenger in the name of the high mass.

My stay in Dresden gave me not only an opportunity of hearing good music, but of becoming acquainted with Mr. John Schneider, organist of the Royal Lutheran church, a gentleman whose talents in organ playing, extempore fugue, and other branches of his art, are highly extolled, but one

THE ORGAN IN THE ROYAL CATHOLIC CHURCH
Has 47 Stops, three Rows of Keys, and Pedals.

HAUPTWERK. (Middle Row.)	OBERWE K. (Upper Row.)	BRUSTWERK. (Under Row.)
1. Principal .... 16 feet	1. Principal ... 8 feet	1. Principal .... 4 feet
2. Cornett ...... 5 ranks	2. Quintatön .. 16 -	2. Gedakt ...... 8 -
3. Bordun ...... 16 feet	3. Unda Maris . 8 -	3. Rohrflöte .... 4 -
4. Rohrflöte .... 8 -	4. Gedakt ...... 8 -	4. Nassat ...... 3 -
5. Quinta ...... 3 -	5. Octava ...... 4 -	5. Octave ...... 2 -
6. Tertia .... 2 -	6. Quintatön .. 8 -	6. Sesquialter aus 2 -
7. Cymbel ...... 3 ranks	7. Rohrflöte ... 4 -	7. Quinta .... 1½ -
8. Trompete .... 8 feet	8. Nassat ...... 3 -	8. Sifflöte ...... 1 -
9. Principal .... 8 -	9. Octave ...... 2 -	9. Mixtur ...... 3 ranks
10. Viola di Gamba 8 -	10. Tertia aus .. 2 -	10. Chalmeaux .. 8 feet
11. Octave ...... 4 -	11. Flageolet .... 1 -	
12. Spitzflöte .... 4 -	12. Mixtur ...... 4 ranks	
13. Octave ...... 2 -	13. Vox humana 8 feet	
14. Mixtur ...... 4 ranks	14. Echo .... 5 ranks	
15. Fagott .... 16 feet	in a closed case.	

PEDAL.

1. Principal Bass .... 16 feet.	Wood.
2. Untersatz .... 32 -	-
3. Pausan .... 16 -	Metal.
4. Trompete .... 8 -	
5. Clarino .... 4 -	
6. Octave Bass .... 8 -	
7. Octava .... 4 -	
8. Mixtur .... 6 ranks	

Besides the Stops are Schwebung, Bass-Ventil, Tremulant, and Klingel.

This organ, Silbermann's masterpiece, was completed and erected in the year 1754. Gottfried Silbermann died during its progress, and it was finished by his nephew John Daniel Silbermann, of Strasbourg, who had assisted him in the work.

with whom fame is, as yet, behindhand, for his merits far exceed the character which is heard of them. In Munich and Vienna I heard much of this gentleman as *the* organist of Germany, and of his brother Mr. F. Schneider, capell-meister in Dessau, who has written several oratorios of great reputation. In Mr. John Schneider I found a pianoforte player of great and unerring execution, with that rare power of mental concentration which is the best characteristic of the extemporaneous faculty. We held a conversation on the German method of organ playing, and agreed that the instrument was, out of all comparison, the most difficult of attainment, as it required that the performer should have all the command of the best pianoforte player, and afterwards that he should attain the organ touch, style, and a facility in the use of the pedals. During my visit Mr. Schneider sat down and extemporized on his pianoforte in a very masterly manner, preluding in C minor, introducing an air with variations in the same key, and concluding with a fugue in the major, all which movements grew out of one another, with a real musician-like inspiration. This will strike many musical readers as being like the off-hand design which Wesley frequently makes, and the resemblance in the mode of thinking was remarkable. For sheer organ playing Schneider is, however, quite alone; the difficulties which he there masters make all ordinary attempts appear child's play in the comparison. I attended him in some private visits to his church, the doors of which were always beset by a dozen musical friends and people who delight in organ playing, where he indulged us with the choral vorspiele of Sebastian Bach, the fugues of the same, and at our request with some MS. variations on the theme " God save the King," composed for the sake of displaying the variety of stops in his instrument. The enthusiastic pleasure with which Schneider plays, makes it tenfold pleasant to see and hear him; he is not like a coxcomb who works hard and affects ease, he is wrapt up in his subject, plays with care, but with no more appearance of effort than necessarily grows out of such attempts.

One morning on which we visited the church, happening to be rather sultry, before beginning to play he whipped off his coat, saying to his company " *Verzeihen sie, meun Herrn*," (Your pardon, gentlemen), and in that pleasant state of unformality plunged into the thick of the Kyries of Sebastian Bach, playing the whole of six and seven real parts with such a towering skill in the pedals

as to make one think the old author returned from
his grave.   Mr. Schneider's manners are as unpretending as his performance is wonderful ; he modestly says, that in order to play the music of Bach
it is necessary to know every bar by heart.   The
rapidity and smoothness with which the *toeing* and
heeling of the pedals are managed, though a great
difficulty, is not so admirable as the power of keeping the thoughts employed in many directions at
once.

M. Klengel, who formerly distinguished himself
as a pianoforte player in London, has, in his retirement at Dresden, completed a work which will be
considered by the musical world as one of the most
masterly of its age or kind ; and it shows him to
have studied the works of Sebastian Bach with
good results.   This performance is a collection of
canons for the pianoforte, containing all the most
difficult models of that difficult and classical species
of composition.   They are intended not only as
studies in playing and writing, and as specimens of
ingenuity and research, but in other respects they
have a fire, fancy, and melodiousness which make
them especially attractive.   I was fortunate enough
to hear M. Klengel play a great part of his collection, and was delighted with the skill he exhibited

in their execution, for where great contrivance is shown in the writing, the difficulty of performance is infinitely enhanced. The regular canon in two parts for the pianoforte, of which many examples are to be found, is no very great achievement; but to produce designs of the augmented, diminished, *per modo contrario*, with good melodies and attractive sequences, show that the genius reigns here and revels in its element. I could not help regarding M. Klengel with feelings of respect and admiration as a professor, who despising the immediate return of money as the reward of his genius, chooses to leave posterity the result of his leisure and thought, and to add another valuable present to the great works his countrymen have already put forth. The study of M. Klengel looks out upon a beautiful country, through windows richly over-canopied with flowering shrubs and broad leaves; its walls are ornamented with the paintings of his father, who was an artist attached to the Saxon court, and as much distinguished in one art as his son in another.

The Italian Opera at the *Linkeschen Bad* gave Rossini's " Italiana in Algieri" among other modern performances. Though the house is insignificant, the company is a good one, and not the worse to my taste for the admission of some German singers to make up a deficiency in number; among these is a soprano, Mademoiselle Veltheim, who bears the palm from all the Italians of the corps. The great difference between the Italian comic opera performed in Germany and England consists in the extravagant fooleries of the buffo, which would be hardly tolerated by our grave London audiences, who, shrouded in their contempt for the ridiculous, will not enjoy the refreshing exquisite laughter it affords. The people of Dresden see the wisdom of occasional nonsense, which is a perception absolutely necessary to the right enjoyment of the Italian comic opera. De Begnis has the face of a weeping Magdalen compared with that of the inimitable Benincasa, a Neapolitan, whose genius for the absurd is unequalled, and whose claims to approbation as a musician and bass singer are far from contemptible.

The chief places of summer evenings' resort in Dresden are the great garden, the garden of the *Linkischen Bad*, and the terrace overlooking the Elbe. At the first of these places the music was generally excellent, and it was my practice on a fine warm afternoon, having dined and duly discussed my glass of Würtzburger, to jump into a fiacre and drive there through pleasant avenues of trees and country houses; and the agreeableness of the ride was not lessened by seeing from time to time groups of handsome girls seated in the green trellised bowers of their gardens, bareheaded, reading or working together—then to leap out of the coach to the first finale in " Figaro," or something as good, and to take coffee seated under the fine old arm of a tree, looking upon the evening sun or the golden clouds about it, surrounded by a throng of happy faces.

This park, which was attached to a royal residence, but is now given up for the gratification of the public, is a most charming place; the trees, instead of being younger than one's self, as they appear at Vienna, look *ancestral* and venerable. The ladies who visit this place very wisely employ their hands in knitting, though I believe from their looks that the manufacture does not absorb much of their thoughts: the gentlemen in the mean time lounge about, recognizing and exchanging amenities with their acquaintances. Great cheerfulness results from this open air existence in Germany; life runs good to the last here, for in no place have I seen so many happy old men, or met with more innocent or steadfast politicians, especially if Eng-

land was the theme of discourse. One of these
used to single me out every day with a fresh eulogium on *Herr* Canning, until the relation of his
virtues became rather tedious. In this garden the
late Weber was in the habit of meeting his friends,
and would sometimes goodnaturedly correct the
band if they misapprehended the style or time of
his airs.—An opinion still prevails in Dresden that
disappointment at the reception of " Oberon " in
England hastened the composer's death—a mistake
as to the fact: and even as far as emolument, and
the caresses of the fashionable world are concerned,
the Germans formed their expectations of his
success from their ignorance of the class of character which is calculated to make a man of genius
the rage in England. The simplicity of manners
which attends conscious talent will not do *alone* for
a drawing-room in Grosvenor Square. When Rossini came among us, he assumed the man of fashion,
and with it a stock of impudence as remote from a
proper degree of self-respect, as the extreme of servility would have been : he could sing, and though
he did not complete the opera which he was to
write in England, his ready pen and ready voice
stood him in good stead, as may be remembered in
the musical lamentations which he composed *extem-*

pore on the death of Lord Byron. On that occasion the *maestro* himself was the mournful jackpudding wailing the loss that was gain to him with the happiest sorrow. By this craft, and by being the nightly *lion* of evening parties, he retired from England in the jovial possession of more thousands of pounds than has ever been acquired by any musician before or since in as many months. Had Weber possessed the same florid health and elastic spirits, and left behind him that baneful quality called modesty, he might have trebled the amount of his contract with the theatre.

As all the actors, singers, and artists of the city frequent this garden, it is neither an unpleasant nor disagreeable occurrence to find oneself seated next to some person who the evening before was filling you and a whole room of company with admiration and pleasure. The applause of the public does not spoil the *bonhommie* of the man, and the repulsiveness of an overweening conceit is unknown. Every talented performer exerts himself to please, receives praise as his due, but forgets the next day to rate himself higher than his neighbour, whose only merit is good nature, and a discreet management of his pipe.

The most noticeable music here given was some

of the sinfonias of Beethoven and Haydn—the overtures to Fidelio and Anacreon, Mozart's finales to Don Juan and Figaro, ably adapted, and the voice parts taken in for a band by Meyer, brother of the celebrated composer of that name. I will not say that this music was so dashingly played as it might have been by our Philharmonic orchestra, but it was complete enough for those who enjoy the display of an author's mind more than the pride of perfect *fiddling.* Our artists play too well, which is a paradox of which the initiated will require no explanation. In this garden it is not unfrequent that concertos or solos on the bass trombone (the pausan, in Germany) are to be heard. The other evening there was a waltz with variations played, which for tone, the rapid tonguing of the notes, and extraordinary shifting, was delightful. On my complimenting the youth who had thus signalized himself, he smiled and said, " It requires good lungs ;" a conviction which had pressed upon me before from seeing his inflated cheeks, and the suffusion of moisture on his skin. The cavity of his chest in supplying this enormous tube must have been at every blast as the exhausted receiver of an air-pump; and the appearance of exertion would have been laughable, had not the effect counteracted any tendency of that sort. It is no more possible to affect ease in an achievement of this kind, than it was for a stout man whom I once saw scrambling up a garden wall to get out of the reach of a mad dog that was pursued in full hue and cry down a country lane.

The music in this garden is played in a kind of open summer-house, and the performers do not scruple during the pauses to avail themselves of certain ham sandwiches and sundry bottles of wine, thus repairing dilapidations of their spirits, and keeping up excitement. I found here a man, named Stephan, a good trumpeter, who had lived for many years at Brighton in the private band of the Prince Regent, but who preferred Dresden in spite of more work and less pay. England he thought a dear country, for, said he, " I must pay six-and-tearty paunds a-year for my leetle hause." Stephan said something more about his wife not liking our climate; but I saw plainly that he loved sociality, and thought our Sundays rather dull.

Those who visit Dresden, and are fond of old romaunts and tales of chivalry, will do well to visit the *Rist Kammer*,* an old time-blackened building, to see those iron suits in which the knights of

* Armoury.

yore rattled forth to an encounter. The collection is large and interesting; one traverses whole suits of rooms in which these empty shells, mounted on chargers, painted and caparisoned to the life, only leave the imagination to bring back the riders, no very difficult task. Some of the armour used in the first wars with the Turks bears indentations of shot, which must have given the wearer a surprising impetus without doing him any injury. One of the rooms exhibits the ghastly portraits of two bashaws killed under the walls of Vienna, with gaping sabre-cuts on their foreheads: they look smiling at their death wounds, grim and insensible. In looking at the walls of mail, I could not help thinking that they must have induced an artificial courage on the wearers, which renders it doubtful how they would have gone into battle in *cuerpo* as the wild Indians, or even in a regimental uniform. The quick re-move which a cannon shot must have made among men in harness, when it only bulged their coats, must have warmed their valour instead of cramping the energies, as it does in these degenerate days. In comparing the elaborate pistol here shown, which followed the diabolical invention of Schwartz, and took a quarter of an hour to fire, with Perkins's steam gun, the most admirable but obvious reflections on the tendency of scientific discovery to produce good out of evil obtrude themselves. The matter-of-fact, mechanical system of shooting, has by degrees abolished all the attributes and trappings of chivalrous warfare: instead of plumed casques, caprioling steeds, and couched lances—all the pageantry which poets delight to describe—we have now a method which makes physical strength and personal prowess of less consequence, and puts it out of the power of a fellow, whose "bulk and big assemblance" is as of a drayman, after inflicting a beating to make love to one's mistress. What the "light weights" must have done in the olden time, except in feats of minstrelsy, it is difficult to conjecture. The fat calves, ample seat, and broad limbs of August der Stark, King of Poland, whose effigies are here preserved, bespeak a knight as doughty a trencherman in hall as in the lists; his substantial frame could hardly have been nourished, like that of Amadis of Gaul, upon tears, sighs, and love reveries, but one must suppose with an occasional plate of beef insinuated between a sob.

From the windows of the *Rist Kammer* is seen a plat of ground on which jousting formerly took place, and where they in friendly rivalry

hoisted one another from the saddle. The shortness of the course is remarkable.

In one of those morning feasts of Sebastian
Bach, in which, though privately concerted with
M. Schneider, we never failed of participators,
that inimitable artist indulged us with some of
those organ fugues which I had not before heard.
Let me instance those in C and F sharp minor, and
in A flat major, of all which the bass parts were
entirely executed with the pedals.

Had I not been an eye-witness of the rolling passages that were thus given by the feet with the
greatest smoothness and certainty, I should still have
been sceptical as to its possibility. This is evidently
the manner in which the author intended them to
be played, and though an adherence to the mere
bass notes may be thought to produce a thin effect
by those who are accustomed to our instruments,
the rich combination and profundity of the pedal

pipes in the German organs entirely prevent it.
That Schneider has not the largest and finest instrument in Dresden is owing to the caprice of fortune, which seldom measures the organ to the
player. What an appendage to a Gothic cathedral
would this professor be, plying his grave harmonies
and massive fugues to a listening crowd in the
choir, a situation in which sight and hearing wind
up the imagination to a pitch of ecstasy ! No lover
of music can enter one of these buildings while
the organ is under good hands, who does not feel
an instant improvement of himself; his lighter
thoughts subside, a loftier vein of contemplation
and an enthusiasm for the sublime succeeds, which
is the happiest of all mental excitement. In the
whole range of art there is no instrument at which
a man can be placed which will sooner make the
distinction between real and pretended skill appear,
and where so much is required in the fingers of
mechanism, so much in the brain of study, so much
of the inventive faculty besides :—perfection here
should decidedly place the performer at the head of
practical musicians. The German method of
accompanying the chorale when the performer is such
a one as Schneider, is a perfect curiosity in the art ;
and though the groundwork of its character, sim-

plicity, is not forgotten, yet as the same melody is often repeated in the service, the able variety of harmony displayed, with the impromptu moving basses or inner parts, make the skilful handling of these tunes a proof of a ready invention and profound knowledge.

Children here are as commonly accustomed to the daily practice of music as with us they are early habituated to writing and reading. The study of singing, as long as their voices last, is made an amusement to them by the droll words which are set to their canons and other exercises. I passed some very pleasant hours in a singing school, where the scholars and preceptor were equally mirthful over their lessons, the boys never failing to count the time when they were to burst in upon their companions with some ludicrous sentence, or some common-place exalted into a mock importance by the gravity of the music. To hear these " babes and sucklings " in a chorus of Handel or Graun, shows that in the old style of church-music there are no treble voices like those boys for producing the devotional effect those masters intended.

On Sunday morning I attended the Catholic church to hear a grand mass by Naumann, who was formerly capell-meister to this place, and was here visited by Dr. Burney, an event which had escaped my memory until a German friend reminded me of it on the spot. When any music of extra pretension is brought forward in this church, the building has the gaiety of a Sunday opera; the galleries are full of critics, many of them military officers, whose judgment and feeling in musical matters I knew to be warrant for their opinions. Naumann's mass in C was played under the superintendence of music-director Rolle, by a select yet large orchestra and choir. This work is composed in the true Handelian church style; its characteristics are gravity in the harmony, and sweetness in the melody; the Benedictus, the last fugue in the Gloria, and other movements, are only not the first of their kind because Mozart has since lived, and has written masses. Naumann's method of putting instrumental accompaniments is derived from Italian models, and in this respect he has an elegance far beyond the age in which he wrote. Naumann lived to enjoy the highest fame as a composer, but to die in a ditch, an end most unbecoming to a man of genius. He was found drowned in a piece of water belonging to a nobleman's park, after taking an evening's walk there; he is supposed to have been attacked by sudden

illness, to have fallen into the water without power
to extricate himself. A custom prevails here of
introducing an instrumental sinfonia of a single
movement into the service; one by Polledro, a
former music-director at this church, was used,
which possessed some spirited passages, though
altogether a common-place production. With the
works of Polledro I was unacquainted, except with
the violin *solo* which Madame Parravicini exhibited
in Vienna; the association did not tend to exalt
their merits in the present instance. The organists
of the Catholic church are Klengel the pianoforte
player, and Schubert; the latter is esteemed to
have but one preludium for all occasions, and in
Germany a musician of *one* idea is held cheap.
Sassaroni, a Roman *castrato*, who belongs to this
choir, was absent during my visit; but the high
encomium which was passed on his style by some
eminent authorities in Dresden does not permit me
to omit his name among the musical curiosities of
the place.

In the region about Dresden, Berlin, Leipsic,
&c. there is no longer the cheap travelling, nor
the luxuries intellectual and sensual which are procured at an easy rate in the south of Germany.
Throughout my whole journey I have never, ex-

cept about the Rhine, found any inclination in the landlords of inns to extortion; but at the government coach-offices, where the king's livery is worn, it behoves the traveller to look after his dollars. At Dresden, having experienced a very dexterous fraud in arranging for some places to Berlin, and met with similar attempts in other establishments, I would advise that too much stress should not be laid on the honesty of these party-coloured heroes, in spite of their cuffs and collars.

My ride to Berlin was performed by *extra* post, with two companions; there were six of these *extra* post-chaises, each containing three or four persons, which, beside the regular *schnell post wagen*, departed from Dresden for the same place, on the same evening; so that when we alighted at an inn to undergo police examinations, to rave for unattainable coffee, or any thing equally refreshing and impossible, the strife, confusion, noise, which was not much mitigated by the greater number understanding as men of business to push for themselves, were unlike any thing I have before witnessed in the country, and certainly not less disagreeable. When so extensive a caravan as this takes its departure, I find that from the scarcity of cattle, and the inability in some places to procure a driver who

has attained to puberty, that more perilous adventures threaten one than the fear of expiring of
thirst at a country inn.   In the most sleepy hours
of the night the care of our chaise devolved upon
a mere infant, the most preposterously puerile of
postillions, who, though stuffed into importance,
and covered with a " thick scurf" of great coat,
jack-boots, horn, &c. could not keep himself awake ;
the protector of our lives and interests did not
trouble himself with needless exertion to avert
those decrees of fate which we expected every
instant to be contemplating in the bosom of some
ditch or more unpleasant river.   Although we had
frequently roused our young guide, the lurch of
his head in a few minutes afterwards showed that
he had relapsed, and our only resource was to keep
him in talk, and the irritated pettish squeak of the
boy's voice ever and anon answering to the deep
authoritative growl of a Hambro' merchant in the
inside, was in ludicrous contrast.   No sooner were
we quit of the blind guidance of the boy, than we
were accommodated with a sober, wakeful man,
and fresh horses, one of which was a stallion, who
did not appear to have been educated in a Stoical
school, for he reared, pawed, kicked, snorted,
shrieked, and flung out, to the great dismay of the

passengers and the prejudice of the coachman's knee-pans, nor did he alter his line of conduct until some poles were brought to cudgel him into humility.

The roads between Dresden and Berlin are now in a course of renovation, and it is well that they should be so, for the deep, heavy ruts of dust that continually impede the horses, have their tedium unrelieved by views or pleasant landscapes, and on this expedition the body is as much macerated by abstinence as the eye fatigued by the monotonous desert. There is one advantage in the Prussian journey which it should not be robbed of in narration, and that is, that the traveller rides smoothly and decorously, whereas in the southern parts, between Augsbourg and Munich, such malignant bumps are inflicted on the inferior part of his person in the many sharp descents and abrupt rises of the roads there, that, seated in a diligence, he is incontinently jerked into the arms of a lady opposite, and finds himself involuntarily discharging an extempore embrace, not more brief than ardent.

The entrance to Berlin is agreeable, though the country is still flat and dusty, except where relieved by kitchen-gardens and moist-looking vegetables.

As for the city itself, it is the longest, most strag-
gling, unsymmetrical, discrepant metropolis that I
have seen—a jumble of magnificent buildings and
ruinous houses, the streets in the best part of the
town broad, the buildings low, alleys in the neighbourhood of palaces, the river a muddy canal.
There is no look of out-of-door enjoyment in
Berlin, but a great confluence of soldiers, porters,
and trades-people in the streets, give them the
bustling appearance of a mercantile town in
England.

BERLIN.

THE German opera-house here is in its size, costly
decorations and embellishments, but little inferior
to that at Munich; the boxes are supported by
cariatides. In the price of admission it approaches
the dearness of the opera in Vienna. When one
of the great works of Gluck is given here, the
house is crowded to the ceiling with a most attentive and judicious audience, which actually bestows
its approbation when a singer executes a passage
with just expression and good taste, rather than
when he exposes himself as a fool. No praise can
be high enough for the Iphigenia in Tauris, as it
is performed in Berlin, whether Gluck's divine
music, the perfect accompanying of the band, or
the skill of the principal singers and *actors* are in
question. I add the last term because there is a
warmth and intensity in their mode of taking recitative, and an energy in their action which nothing
but such music as Gluck's could inspire. I had
almost forgotten, in listening to this natural and

astonishing work (where the passion seems of itself
to have found its expression in music as justly and
more intensely than it could be conveyed by the
perfection of language), that such a style could
possibly be misunderstood and disliked ; and it is
a sad feeling to wake out of the voluptuous dream
of melancholy and tenderness in which such heart-
felt modulation wraps the listener, to the thought
that this great master, with all his store of human
sympathies and profound intimacy with the sweetest
yearnings of our nature, should have lived only
for one little capital in the north of Europe.

Gluck is the only composer of operas who in a
plot, of which every feature is serious, has so diver-
sified his movements and subjects as to keep the
interest ever alive ; in spite of a tendency to gloomy
sublimity and sorrowful emotions, he kept his
thoughts out of the enchanted circle, and wandered
onwards, instead of lingering enamoured about some
favourite phrases.   He is the only master capable
of grappling with a classical subject; he could
give us, better than any,

> " Ariadne passioning for Theseus' injury
>   And unjust flight."

No lovers, tyrannically separated for ever, have the
despair of his.   His operas are *truly* grand, not in

the modern sense, because the heroes wear helmets and the heroines tiaras, but because every tender phrase and declaration echoes from the deepest recesses of the heart. Gluck was so much in earnest, so exquisitely melodious, so fanciful in his accompaniments, so pure in his harmonies, so rich and unexpected in his modulation and transition, that all must acknowledge in him the precursor and model of Mozart; besides, there is a solidity in his love of good sequences, for which I must confess (and with me most musicians) a sneaking kindness. One who had only heard the Vestale of Spontini would hardly believe it possible to produce so great an effect as Gluck has done in his disposition of three soprani voices in the chorus of priestesses in this opera.

Of the Iphigenia of Mademoiselle Scheckner I cannot speak with any feeling short of rapture: a better voice, a more chastened style both in recitative and song, has never been heard on the stage— besides she has faith in the capability of Gluck. This *prima donna* is about eighteen years of age, and a visitor at Berlin from Munich: she is a beautiful girl, who gives up all her young enthusiasm to music, without an atom of that self-sufficiency which is too frequently taken for science.

During the whole of this arduous attempt, I did not detect a single false intonation—which by the bye was lucky, for the pit and boxes in Berlin are enormously critical, and can tell wrong notes from right ones. In the prayer, "O du die mir das leben gab" (O thou who gav'st me life), she poured forth her whole soul; and it is one of those in the character of which Gluck particularly excels.

That good music makes good singing, good acting, that self-forgetfulness and total absorption in the scene which conveys the truest delight to the observer, I have also to remark in M. Rebenstein and M. Stümer. The first of these (Orestes) showed himself a tolerable singer, and played his part with wonderful spirit; the second (Pylades) is the most charming tenor I have heard in Germany, more particularly as to his style and feeling. Nothing can be more finely conceived by a composer than the devoted friendship here existing: the air sung by Pylades, in the second act—

"But one wish, one desire, have I with thee, dear friend,"

contains the excess of a womanly tenderness. For dramatic variety and relief, the opera contains the bass songs of Thoas, King of Tauris, which are full of fire and grandeur, but being not well sung, the performer was laughed at; the chorus of demons and furies, interspersed with recitative, in the second act, is fearful; the marches and chorus of Scythian barbarians have a wildness of character which shows the untired inexhaustible invention of the composer. In the accompaniment of the voice, especially in recitative, the Berlin orchestra might be the pattern of any in Europe.

Before the commencement of the opera the stage was crowded with a vast wind-instrument band and chorus (numbering about three hundred performers), which, with the assistance of the regular orchestra, and directed by four maestri di capella, with Spontini at their head, gave a composition in honour of a court birth-day. The groundwork of this music was " God save the King;" but the simple tune was interlarded with long instrumental symphonies, which were quite irrelevant to its style and character. This noisy parade of loyalty was intended by Spontini to please the king of Prussia, whose ear is obtuse, except to an immense crash, and the only objection to it was, that the musician had, in gratifying his royal patron, forsaken consistency and good taste without necessity to have done so.

One of those institutions most honourable to the

enthusiasm and spirit of the musical amateurs of Berlin is the foundation of its singing school, the whole expense of the edifice in which the practice is conducted, and every contingency, being defrayed out of the pockets of the musical public. The singing school is a handsome white building, standing near the university, and in the neighbourhood of the famed walk of linden trees; it contains three hundred regular students, and accommodation on public days for an audience of seven hundred. There is no band. The resident professor here is M. Zelter, a tall silver-haired old gentleman, of bland manners, and whose skill as a master is well attested by the proficiency of his scholars. Such a chorus as this will never be found in any part of the world until the same number of young people has the same opportunities of rehearsing together, and consequently of understanding a composer in the gross as well as in detail. The difficulty of the vocal pieces I heard executed here might have appalled the most resolute and experienced of sight-singers.

The whole of Spohr's mass for two choirs and ten voices was sung with as much nicety of tune as though it had been played by a band of instruments; and it is not the easiest composition which might be selected to try a chorus, for the music abounds with enharmonic transitions and learned modulations. As all expectation of hearing this work performed as the author intended it at any concert in London would be utterly vain, the value of this opportunity, which enables me to form some estimate of Spohr's claims to distinction as a church writer, is enhanced. The novelty and ambition of the attempt, which is to employ the refinements of the modern style of harmony and melody upon vocal and sacred music, is in itself good, but the effect it produces is inferior to that expectation which a view of the careful disposition of its parts raises in the mind. It is too chromatic for church music; grandeur is always sacrificed for the sake of showing some new or unexpected mode of harmonizing a passage. The German critics complain that Spohr will not leave a melody to itself, but by continually endeavouring to improve it with some novelty of accompaniment, destroys the sentiment: this charge is in some sort just, but the fault is on the right side in instrumental composition, which is evidently the tendency of Spohr's genius; his melodies are fit to *sing* on the violin, but are not fit for the voice. Of this mass the fugue, " Cujus regni non erit finis," produced the best effect; the movement with *soli* voices, and an accompanying chorus at the " Agnus Dei," is constructed on the instrumental model, and is not so good as it is new.

I had now time to draw a comparison between the results of the modern school of writing and that of Handel, whose Utrecht Te Deum followed in the rear of Spohr's mass : and I was amused to hear in the *verses* of this composition that disposition of the voices in suspensions upon a moving bass, and complete imitation of our English cathedral style, which Handel, who never failed from conscience qualms to adopt what he liked in other persons, learned during his residence among us. Of this the Germans are not the least aware, and admire that in him which belongs to hands of whose existence they have no notion.

It will scarcely admit of question, that the pleasure conveyed by Handel, our anthem writers, and the old masters of Italy, in sacred harmony, is tenfold greater than in modern attempts, though the latter appear extremely elaborate. The fugue, that noble pillar of church music, is the point where the moderns are at fault : their subjects are too self-evident; they have none of that " happy alchymy of mind " which turns a common phrase into an invaluable sequence ; nor does one discover in the artful creeping in of one point upon the heels of another, in the distribution and mixture of the subjects, that consummate skill and thought which in the old writers shows how they must have revolved and re-considered their respective bearings.

All the choral pieces performed at this academy are accompanied on the pianoforte by one of the pupils of M. Zelter—the professor leisurely striding about the room accelerates or retards the time where such correction is necessary. There is no pleasanter peculiarity about the singing school than the sight of sixty or seventy young ladies heartily employed on a motett of Palestrina, Mozart, or Sebastian Bach, and enjoying the music: such solid acquirements of knowledge and taste as this power implies, make those drawing-room exhibitions, to which their skill in playing or singing has been hitherto chiefly devoted, appear too poor and un-worthy a destination for female talent.

At the König Städtisches Theater (there are three here in constant play) Mademoiselle Sontag is the presiding deity—the goddess of the students and the Vestris of Berlin: and few there are whose hearts are fenced with such impenetrable buff as to rebel against her sovereignty, or refuse to adore. When the lady plays, the doors and lobby of the

theatre are beset by all the wild youths of the city,
each of whom would consider himself a traitor to
the cause of beauty if he did not contribute all that
in him lay to make the entrance as much like a
bear-garden as possible : there is no such thing as
attaining to a song here but at the expense of
mobbing, rib-squeezing, and considerable condensation of the person.   Those who expect to find in
Mademoiselle Sontag a musical genius, will be disappointed : nor do I think her fame would have
reached England, had it not been for certain circumstances of gossip unconnected with her profession.   The lady is of middling height, well formed,
with fair hair, and a set of little features which
have a kind expression in them.   To venture upon
elaborate praise of the complexion and shape of an
actress, as it may involve a eulogium on the per-
fumer or staymaker which is not intended for those
worthies, would be imprudent as well as presumptuous.   Mademoiselle Sontag has a pleasant quality
of voice, with a small quantity of tone in it, but
with plenty of flexibility ; an endowment which she
displays so frequently, that if one could but check
the fluttering, unstaple, whimsical little creature, a
long breathing clear note would be invaluable.   Her
highest praise is said to be, that she sings Rossini's

music perfectly, and joins to this great *naïveté* in her acting, and that such qualifications for a performer are seldom found in company.

In a French opera by Auber, of which the German version is called Der Schnee (The Snow), Mademoiselle Sontag turns the heads of the whole town: in this piece the audience is charmed with every flourish, enraptured with every look, movement, or gesture; and as to her playfulness, it is seen with ecstasy. The fact is, that Mademoiselle Sontag is not tried at the severe tribunal of the German opera in Berlin, but sings at a theatre where three parts of the people come to see her alone, and among her admirers are certainly not to be reckoned those whose judgment in musical matters is of the clearest. The dispassionate unprejudiced listener discovers little more to admire in her roulades than he has heard hundreds of times in those of other singers. Mademoiselle Sontag has a distinct articulation, and deals in all the minutiæ of refinement; but in a sustained *cantabile*, that sort of movement in which the soul of the singer looks out, she is lamentably deficient. It is the leaven of Catalani's bad style which has deteriorated the taste of the present day, and directly opposes it to a simple and natural mode of expression.

Spontini enjoys in this capital an enviable situation in point of emolument, and an easy one as to duties—about 600*l.* a-year for manufacturing an opera occasionally. His Alcidor, and La Vestale, are performed here with the utmost magnificence ; and the king, who likes a grand *spectacle*, and judges of music by its loudness, is not very difficult to please. I cannot join in the encomiums which are here bestowed on the works of this writer even by the same people who by an unaccountable, but not unusual perversity, praise Gluck and Mozart. Spontini's melodies are often trite ; he neither interests one by the purity and elegant turn of his airs like Paisiello, nor does he keep the attention awake by eccentric and ingenious accompaniments like Weber ; he too frequently mistakes mere wilfulness and a love of surprising his audience for originality. As Spontini was decoyed here from Paris, there is a prejudice in his favour, for every thing which comes from that city is esteemed in Germany, and the claims of the Parisians to arbitration in matters of taste are considered indisputable.

The other evening, in the play-house, I was so fortunate as to hear Paisiello's charming opera, La Molinara (Die Schöne Müllerin) performed with as much spirit as it was in London during the supremacy of Naldi. What complete simplicity, yet what genius, pervades the whole of this composition: the melodies so unpretending and pure, the accompaniments delicate and fanciful, yet possessing fascination for those who are accustomed to the most learned combinations. Paisiello has that indefinable charm in his writings which causes us to listen with delighted attention, when more refined harmony and melody would frequently tire; with him the propriety of the sentiment is ever so admirable that he never " o'ersteps the modesty of nature." The songs of La Molinara were sung with good taste by Madame Seidler; but the concerted music, in which the unfortunate maiden with her pestering and intriguing lovers are either quarrelling or kissing, each trying to delude the other, kept me in an agony of laughter and delight. The singers here are infatuated with the drollery of their parts, and give themselves up to the fooling of the hour body and soul. It is when music hurries the feelings along with it in one impetuous stream, when actors and audience are animated by the same frenzy, that the dramatic composer triumphs, then he shows us his divine commission to delight under the hand and seal of genius.

The great German harmonists, Bach and Handel,

(who have rendered Saxony famous as the cradle in which those Newtons of the science were nurtured), seem yet to have left in the north of Germany an atmosphere peculiarly favourable to the production of that rarity—a good organist.   In the church of St. Mary there is in this capacity a scion of the illustrious stock of Sebastian.   M. Bach is a young man of frank and cordial manners, and a very clever artist, as I had reason to know in an evening's organ-playing which I enjoyed with a party at his church. Though the lovers of that great master Sebastian Bach are here, as in England, the select and under-standing few, there is an intensity in their adoration of his sequences which is ten times worth the ap-plause of a fashionable concert room.   Here up-lifted hands, glistening eyes, voices which must break forth into singing, confess that the soul floats delighted on that flood of harmony.   Praise of the writing is not attempted, words are too cold ; but there is never-ending admiration of the mind which made all melodies bend to its will, and serve its purposes in the higher, lower, middle regions of sound.   It was this man, who being once sent for by the king, came before him blushing and confused as a maiden, but for whose empire over sounds I think it would be easy to lay down a sceptre.

The German organists are strong muscular men ; a lady performer (unless she were of Amazonian stock) would be a phenomenon. Music requires strange qualifications for its professors ; for instance, an organist should have the bodily thews of a porter, conjoined with a sensibility which that rough state of the animal seems to preclude. The history of Handel reconciles so many apparent contradictions, that it is difficult to know what is not compatible. After battling with Cuzzoni, and treating the whole sex with the imperiousness and indifference of a bashaw, he could write a tender air ; although a great eater and drinker, as well as enormously sedentary, from devotion to his art, he kept his brain clear and his ideas free, could plan his immortal choruses, extemporize without stagnation of thought ; the dull fumes of sensual indulgence left him untouched ; the business of engaging singers, travelling, attending rehearsals, &c. the commonplaces of a musician's life, could not stop the grand operations of his poetic genius. With the partial knowledge the public of Germany have as yet of Handel, his fame rings from one end of the country to another ; but when the full blaze of his glory is revealed by his great work, Israel in Egypt, his memory will be perfectly idolized.

The principal Catholic church here is small, and not handsome. In the interior it resembles the Frauen's Kirche in Dresden, which presents a large rotunda with rows of circular galleries reaching to its ceiling ; it is a building better adapted for concerts or theatrical exhibitions than for religious purposes. The organ here is contemptibly small, and the choir weak. In the Lutheran church of St. Nicholas is an instrument with diapasons as soft and round as any built by old Green. So much of the finery of the altar, so many pictures and gilt crucifixes are left in the Lutheran churches, precisely in the same situations as they occupied during the reign of the Catholics, that it is often difficult to know at first sight for which service the place is appropriated, unless the portrait of Luther set the matter at rest. The French soldiers have done infinite mischief to the churches in Berlin, by using them, as they did the cathedral of Cologne, for stables ; and for this wicked insult the Prussians will never forgive them.

In the Protestant cities of the north of Germany, upon the death of any individual, the ceremony is observed of sending a number of little boys in black cloaks and cocked-hats, to stand in a semi-circle before the house of the deceased, to sing a brief and brisk kind of death-psalm, but the effect is almost ludicrous. To hear the merry shrieking of these little thoughtless imps the first thing on waking in the morning, is the most disagreeable *memento mori* imaginable.

All the common soldiers in Berlin are allowed on certain afternoons in the week to perambulate if they choose the Museum of Anatomy, a regulation which appears a monstrous perversion of its scientific uses; but on the Continent the sight of dissections, abortions, and old bones, affords infinite pleasure to all classes. In Amsterdam, during the fair, I found the market-women paying their stivers to be made learned in osteology, the venerable lecturer in the Museum dividing his attention between his skeletons, his audience, and some soup that was cooking on the fire, the last not the least of his cares.

The Kunst Kammer, a museum of natural curiosities, I found worth seeing, more for the sake of the ingenious exhibitor than even for the rarities themselves. The keeper of this place, in showing a set of Indian weapons to a party of ladies, did not content himself with coldly giving their names and uses, but sticking a plume of coloured feathers on his head, twitching a mantle round him, and

catching up a lance, he became the chief of an
Indian tribe in the act of darting upon his enemy;
the expression of his face changing with his character, I could not recognize in the straddling en-
thusiast before me, the indifferent man of office
with whom we are acquainted in England. Even
as far north as Berlin, German blood runs brisk
and sprightly.

One distinguishing characteristic of the excellence of this country in music is the skill of the
wind-instrument bands, and the nicety of tune
with which they play pieces containing the most
learned modulation. At a concert in the open air
I heard a fantasia of Mozart in C minor (to be
found in his pianoforte works)

very effectively arranged by Neithardt; a finale
from the Zauberflöte of the same; the overture to
the Berg König, by Lindpainter; with some lighter
pieces and horn music. The complete *accord* with
which some very difficult enharmonic changes were
accomplished by this numerous and magnificent
band, showed great knowledge in the arranger and
skill in the performers, a perfection, the value of
which, is known only to those who are aware of

the unmanageable nature of wind-instruments. I found here many young lads who had attained great eminence as practical musicians, and with it (a rare thing to discover among those who associate in large societies) they joined a simplicity of manners and modest behaviour which were in the highest degree attractive. Two of these youths played some variations for two clarionets by Kästner, and another the corno *principale* in an overture for horns by Neithardt, of which last the effort was perfectly extraordinary. The ingenuity of the German horn music is completely unimaginable by those who have never heard any, as it presents some of the most curious discoveries of modern combination, with a tone of the richest quality. Neither is the music so simple or so much restrained to one key as might be fancied ; the thoughts of the composer are not screwed down by this or that apparent impossibility, but the composition flows on as though it were written for instruments presenting the usual facilities.

Though the Germans have a tendency to the enjoyment of luxurious indolence, they are most unremittingly diligent in acquiring mechanical skill, and are always exporting to England some new professor, who has practised for so many hours

a day more than the one who came before him ; so
that, in the present day, he who can best dispense
with sleep has the best chance of success.

When a piece is concluded at a concert here, the
many persons who crowd about the director, anxious
to speak with him, either commending, blaming, or
remarking upon the beauties of the composition,
show how much the science is valued and cultivated.
There is none of that heart-sickening, cold, dead
silence at the end of a fine movement, which makes
one feel indignant that good music should be
thrown away ; for to play a sinfonia of Mozart or
Beethoven to some audiences is much about the
same as exhibiting a picture of Rembrandt to a
clown ; while at the same time there is none of that
violent applause of individual performers which
akes them lose sight of the goodness of music in
the vapours of self-admiration.   In England the
Italian method of *bravoing* an author might sometimes be adopted at concerts with good effect.

Inferior as the generality of the violin and pianoforte players (Hummel, Mayseder, and Spohr the
exceptions) are to our own, the dillettanti of Germany, a very numerous body, afford an ample evi-
dence of the bent of the national genius.   I have
had much pleasure in hearing the improvisation of

some of this class, who understood the art of modulation surprisingly well for amateurs. I will not say that the fantasia which they will sometimes amuse a company with is sufficiently restrained in its thinking and symmetrical in its features to be dignified with the appellation of *extempore* playing, yet still the knowledge of harmony which is shown in stringing chords well together, and the intimacy with the bearings of remote keys, make them the best possible of critics. The amateurs in Berlin are all little *maestri ;* they dabble in composition, and have most of them the score of a mass, sinfonia, or overture locked up in their desks, the consciousness of which helps to sweeten their lives, and gives them the smiling self-satisfaction which Mr. Bickerstaff discovered in the girl who wore embroidered garters. The question is not answered in Berlin as it used to be with us—" Is Mr. ———— musical ? " " Yes, he plays a *little* on the flute :" after which the wary inquirer would be sure to avoid a demonstration of the fact. But the answer might run thus : " Yes, he plays Sebastian Bach, sings at sight, and has written a set of quintetts."

Mademoiselle Scheckner has, in sustaining the first part of a one act opera, entitled Cordelia, done more for her reputation as a singer than even

by her performance in Gluck's opera.   The music
of this piece, which is by Kreutzer, more resembles
one impassioned scena for a soprano than an opera;
it is in a very grand style of composition, and very
nearly an hour long.   In a girl only eighteen years
old I have never met with any attempt so arduous
and so successful; and the last is owing entirely to
her having an intense perception of her author's
meaning, and a total destitution of vanity and
affectation.

WITTENBERG—DESSAU.

THE glory of Wittenberg has passed: its once famed university is now merged into that of Halle; its substantial burgers no longer exist. There is nothing to disturb the eternal quiet of this decayed town, except the rattling of the Leipsic diligence, which passes through it once a day, creating a momentary bustle, and some wonderment for the girls at the fountains.

Here is a dilapidated old church, which has its walls covered with the effigies of armed warriors and pious kneeling dames, whose features are rendered by the force of rains and storms dim and almost undistinguishable, and the building itself looks as if it could not support existence much longer.

At one extremity of the town stands a convent of monks, still tenanted, though in the midst of a Protestant country; and in the fields, a little beyond, is the cemetery, so that the poor beadsmen have not far to walk for their graves. The Stadt

Haus is enriched with various relics, as well as ornamented with the portrait of that stout combatter with Satan, and good musician, Martin Luther. Here may be seen the remains of that drinking-cup, out of which, by deep draughts, the reverend father invigorated his faith, and enabled himself to cope with his ghostly enemy; and the portentous double chin which the portrait shows, proves that he considered a reformation in the article of bibacity not indispensable. In an apartment of the Stadt Haus the faces of all the spiritual heroes of the Reformation are still extant in dingy paintings by Lucas Cranach. The pale, thoughtful, ascetic countenance of Melancthon is a complete contrast to the strength and sensuality of Luther's; yet there can be no doubt that the last is he who would best stand the brunt of clashing opinions, and display promptness in arguing or fighting as the occasion might require. Luther has, in rooting out Catholic superstition from the north of Germany, left that part of the country little happier for the change. The preachers of his doctrines seem but scantily attended, and those who visit a Lutheran church may see that the greater part of the congregation are quite indifferent to what is going forward. In Catholic dominions the people are hearty in their prayers, and come from mass lively and cheerful; here they are cold in their religion, and cold in their pleasures. In Antwerp, where may be seen walking the streets a parcel of uncharitable-looking old women arrayed in black cloaks and hoods, the vouchers for their sanctity—in Munich and Vienna, where the dirty monks may be seen by dozens, and wax dolls, far-thing candles, and Aves and Credos are thought to lay up treasure in heaven for the believer—the spirit of enjoyment is universal. The priests among the Catholics personally encourage sight-seeing, and in Vienna they are not squeamish as to the nature of them. They go to plays, speculating on the vanity and foppery of the world, and to ballets, watching there the movements of the per-formers' legs, and gathering instruction. They neither laugh nor speak, but gaze intently.

No part of Wittenberg is more interesting than its picturesque cemetery; the flowers that grow there might vie in beauty with the trimmest par-terre. I found it not unpleasant to stroll into this secluded spot of an evening, while the gnats in a " wailful choir " were swarming in the last rays of the sun: it was easy to find a shady and convenient seat under the young trees, in planting which, kind friends have sought to take out the sting from death; and the sounds of rural life which occasionally interrupted the silence, rendered the contemplative mood the sweeter. A visit to this sort of place appears to me a wholesome discipline of humanity.

About Wittenberg the country is flat and arid. Here and there the noise of the carriage-wheels startled a heron from his patient employment at the edge of a river, who forthwith rose, flagging his wings, and as quickly resettled.

The neighbourhood of Dessau is beautiful, having such fine oaks and park scenery about it as would not disgrace England. In this fertile spot, which becomes a paradise from the barren wilderness with which it is environed, dwells M. Friedrich Schneider, a celebrated capell-meister in the service of the duke, who has written some oratorios now in great reputation in Germany. Rural tranquillity and leisure enable this gentleman to devote himself to church compositions with an ardour which, corresponding with his talents and opportunities, will leave his name an undying inheritance. The Lutheran service here, as in Leipsic, employs a full orchestra; and as every week rehearsals of various sinfonias, motetts, &c. take place, Mr. F.

Schneider enjoys the same advantages for the study of instrumental effect that Haydn did in the service of Prince Esterhazy. The completion of six or seven long choral works, all good, attest a great fund of invention at a time when Handel, Haydn, and Mozart have ransacked the various subjects of fugue, the different modes of accompaniment, or models of design; so that now to produce a distinctive character in composition, is alone a mark of genius. It is no slight task for a composer of the present day to avoid stumbling upon the thoughts of other people. Mr. F. Schneider has written an oratorio to the words of a German translation of Milton, a subject which was attempted in this country by Mr. M. P. King, but without particular success. This work has been given in Berlin, Magdeburg, &c. with the greatest applause; and the author modestly says, that in pursuing the style he does, his desire is to produce something which may please, and yet not experience the early neglect of opera music. Comparison with his great precursors he disclaims, but in my opinion unnecessarily, as my eyes and ears have already convinced me that he is a richly gifted and profound musician. I accompanied this professor into his church at Dessau, to hear the tone of a new organ,

which pleased me by showing that the art of building is not yet forgotten in Germany.   Mr. F.
Schneider is not, like his brother, wholly devoted
to organ-playing, yet his performance is admirably
full and smooth ; he has much command of the
pedals, and mixes five or six parts together with
great contrapuntal knowledge; and this kind of
thick playing, so congenial to the character of the
organ, is precisely what might be expected from
one habituated to choral composition.

It is a general lament among the composers of
Germany, particularly those who put forth voluminous and classical works, that the publication of
their scores is rendered impracticable on account
of the scanty number of purchasers ; hence that
more than half their design remains locked up in
the original ; in this respect they labour under the
disadvantages of the English musician, but then
the absence of teaching, the cheapness of living,
the seclusion of their lives, undisturbed by the
grinding of barrel organs, or the din of Pan's pipes
and ballad-singers, these are the opportunities for a
composer, one who, contemning the voice of popular
applause, feels the highest reward of his labour in
the love of producing good things.

The Duke of Dessau, with that good nature

which characterises the government of the petty states I have visited, throws open his gardens, and admits the public under the windows of his palace. I envy this young nobleman the pleasure he must enjoy in giving a man of genius and industry all possible scope for the exercise of his talent.

LEIPSIC.

In Leipsic, on Saturday mornings, the motetts of the late excellent music-director Schicht are performed by a large chorus. I attended a trial of this sort held in St. Thomas's church, and well thronged with students and other young men, who migrated with extreme and laughable rapidity when the music gave place to the tones of a clergyman. The practice of attempting choruses and fugues in the modern style, entirely without accompaniment, may be calculated to make singers sure of their parts, but it is not so pleasing as when the organ is used to give a binding and weighty effect to the voices. Here that instrument is only used for preluding and interluding, and for the latter the organist very ingeniously carries on the subject which the voices have just quitted. After hearing the admirable mixture which a grand fugue sung, and accompanied on the organ, produces, when the accompanyist is a good one, I am surprised that nothing of the kind is to be heard in Germany.

The instrument in St. Thomas's church is placed too near the ceiling, but its tone is integrally bad.

Those who would conceive an accurate idea of the appearance of Leipsic, with its gable-ended houses and narrow streets, may well consult Prout's excellent drawings of ancient German towns. It is a little heart, with a strong pulse of life beating in it. The exhilarating hilarity of this place may be well enjoyed on the morning of a market-day, when the concourse of regular and earnest buyers and sellers, of girls in pairs, with baskets on their arms, full of adventures and anecdotes, of students who study casuistry to vanquish and overthrow their conscience scruples, make that sea of heads, the mixed costume and variety of colours, one of the most entertaining of sights.

Some apology is absolutely due to the maidens of Leipsic for attempting to commemorate their prettiness, frankness, and politeness in so vulgar a material as prose; there is no city of Germany in which goddesses are so gregarious, scarcely a common female face is to be seen there. Among many of the citizens' daughters, as they appear at market, Fielding might pick out a German copy of his Fanny. They have no impudence of look. They walk out bareheaded with their thick and long hair always beautifully clean, and turned up after the Grecian fashion, fresh and healthy, with handsome features, fine eyes, and in a neat and trim dress of well-selected colours.

The Leipsic people are laughed at in Germany for their mode of softening down their language in speaking (which is by the imitator generally exaggerated into a kind of song) ; but this is not unpleasant, and I have heard nothing which approaches so near to a certain dove-like *cooing* in sound, as the German in the mouth of a Leipsic lady. What it may be in a peroration I do not know, but *sotto voce*, and in the conversational style, it is almost as good as Italian. The theatre here, which is also the opera-house, is suburban, neither very large, rich in its company, nor extensive in its band. Good music is however patronized in Leipsic, for it has lately given the Fidelio of Beethoven, the Don Juan, Zauberflöte, and Seraglio of Mozart, besides Rossini's operas, which, turned into German, with dialogue instead of the recitative, are everywhere stock-pieces. The condition of the people in the pit is not ameliorated by the company of any women, mere rows of men's heads and broad-cloth have in it a black and gloomy appearance. No audience is more critical than this

one, or apt to hiss with extremer violence if ladies
or gentlemen on the stage expose themselves by
attempting too much. I was sorry to find that
Mademoiselle Marschner, from Cassel, in playing
Rossini's Tancred, incurred this ungallant sibilation;
but if screaming renders such conduct justifiable,
I will not undertake to defend her. It is always
unfortunate for a singer when the audience, at the
conclusion of a song, instead of being struck with
admiration, burst out into loud laughter, the more
vulgar part mimicking and hissing; and though in-
capable of joining in this, I could not hear some
staccato passages which were like the fast *quacking*
of a frightened, overdriven duck, without feeling
extremely flushed and uncomfortable. Although
in great cities a very ceremonious and delicate public must not be expected, the lady might as well
have been left to the punishment of failure and
her own reflections.

At the Lutheran church of St. Nicholas, the
dress of the preacher, in a broad starched ruff and
black velvet cap, transported me back to the days of
our own church worthies; yet the congregation,
part of which was employed in sleeping, another
part in watching the exit and entrance of any who
visited the church, paid but a slender compliment

to his eloquence. Here the town's-people settle their spiritual affairs without troubling themselves with an excess of gravity or much puritanical length of face. After attending a service so rigidly shorn of all unholy and sensual gratifications, for Lutheran music has a studied simplicity, one finds less of the street-parading and holiday-making look which makes a Catholic city full of gaiety on Sunday; but within doors there goes forward a joviality which is either much like trespassing, or a *conscientious* neglect of church duties. Never, sitting in my own apartment, or walking out, have I heard more unheavenly sounds of *fiddling*, more roaring of four or five part songs, more thumping of pianofortes, than in Leipsic on Sunday. The students of the university are the principal offenders against the repose of the town on a Sabbath, as at the opera-house they are ever the sturdiest demanders of silence when any sudden eruption of talk makes a passage inaudible. They are a proud, honourable-minded, and obliging set of *harum-scarum* fellows, made up of that warmth of disposition and independence of character, the overflow of which is in youth always pleasant. They are indeed the " blest tobacco-boys," if the day-dreams and visionary plans which the use of that weed inspires, lead to

exertion and completion as well as castle-build-
ing. No one will quarrel with the indolence of
thinking, and the indulgence of thick-coming
fancies while life is all in prospect, difficulties
to be overcome, and great works to be accomplished, but are too much thrall to a long
pipe, and the charms of cool smoke. The
devotion for tobacco is here no *sham* or affectation, but a real, downright, hearty national infa-
tuation—the air seems impregnated with the smell.
The clerk, whose hands are engaged in engrossing,
smokes, holding his pipe between his teeth, the
bowl of it resting some yards off in a window seat.
The postillion, whom the disentanglement of a
contumacious knot in a package obliges to quit his,
lays it down as he would surrender his heart's blood,
with a dismal groan. The students, more gentle
and book learned, make more ingenious and acceptable sacrifices to their Indian god: sixteen of them
came here, occupying the diligence, from Halle,
each armed with his pipe and store of ammunition;
they sat with the windows closed, that the valued
fume might not escape, puffing away, and revelling
delighted. How exquisite must have been the suf-
focation! As it has been said that a quaker's nature
would be a drab-coloured one, so would a German

youth forswear hydrogen and oxygen for an atmosphere compounded of tobacco. The inhabitants of the town are so well accustomed to the freaks and pranks of the university lads, that they pass over any uproar in the streets which calls a stranger to his chamber window, merely saying to the inquirer, with a toss of the head, " Oh! its only the students ! "

No theatrical composer is heard here with so much pleasure as Weber, in praise of whose Oberon the warmest expressions are eagerly lavished. It is a treat to hear the care and correctness with which the opera is given, to make up for what is thought its bad success in England; but the principal singers are far from praiseworthy. The melo-dramatic music used on the stage in accompanying the ascent and descent of the fairy king is so deliciously played, that it might fitly usher in celestial beings. Leipsic has the credit of having first brought forward this opera of Weber, an undertaking which frightened other managers, on account of the expense of scenery, machinery, &c. Those who have witnessed the performance of Oberon at Covent Garden Theatre and that of Leipsic, will, while they give the first the preference for magnificence of decoration, find many points on which even the property-man of the latter may triumph. The music of the band and chorus is decidedly better executed. As it is a piece in which the eye is interested at least as much as the ear, it may not be irrelevant to remark, that the sea-storm here would defy the oldest theatrical boatswain to remember a better. The lightning manufacturer, instead of commonplace resin flashes which the fancy refuses to own, gives all those slight coruscations, those pauses and quick successions, with such an imitation of the colour of the electric fluid, that show him to have watched nature and the warring of the elements. The summoning of the spirits produces an effect any thing but magical : a number of grotesque faces and death's-heads, appearing and vanishing at intervals by means of a transparency, is poor in comparison with the palpable and torch-bearing genii of Covent Garden ; but to make amends, there is none of that risk of life, limb, and expectations which the flying cherubim among us nightly undergo, no little darlings upwhirled aloft to please grave heads in the pit. It has always appeared to me shameful that children, who are not aware of what the state of their feelings would be upon the crack of a string, and their consequent attraction to the centre of gravity, should be so prostituted. To

see Farley and others, who have arrived at years of
discretion, flying across the house by a rope, enact-
ing perhaps the part of some huge obscene bird,
would give pain to nobody. In Leipsic there is
performed, as belonging to the original score of this
opera, a movement with violin *obligato*, and two or
three pieces which I believe have not appeared in
London.

The most richly talented German musicians are
not like those of our own country, who appear once
now and then, like comets, and are almost as difficult of access as it would be to reach one ; foreign
artists of the highest class are as little chary of
their playing as the most unimportant. Here, in
one of the suburban gardens, may be occasionally
heard the famed trombonist M. Queisser, by his
townsmen vaunted the greatest performer of the
whole empire. He is himself the proprietor of this
rural retreat, having captivated the affections and
wedded the form of its female possessor, thus en-
ticing the inhabitants to discuss his viands, and en-
hancing his fortune, as host, by means of his music.
I have heard nothing so soft, round, and deep as
the tone of this extraordinary player, who has, at
the age of twenty-seven, attained the most surprising mastery. At the last music meeting in Zerbst

he performed a concertino on his instrument, which will not be soon forgotten. The palm of excellence for the *knack* in the management of wind instruments must certainly be given to Germany : in this performer there was no appearance of exertion, and the horrors of apoplexy with which swollen veins and starting eyes fill one in ordinary players, were here wholly dismissed from the mind.

From the balcony of the ancient Stadt-Haus in Leipsic the inhabitants are regaled three mornings in a week with an instrumental concert, which is played by the town musicians purely for the amusement of the citizens. Perhaps the magistrates who instituted this regulation were influenced by Shakespear's idea, that the love of music keeps people honest; at all events it is pleasant to find such a sauce sweetening the dry counting-house negotiations, the agreements, contracts, and acceptances which occupy the time of this mercantile city. We may read of certain merchant sailors in the olden time, who when they, in the course of a voyage, came upon a green island, insisted upon quitting their ship and spending a day in dancing and carousing : these people could no more possess our notions of discipline, than German merchants be naturally imbued with the love of money-getting.

If the English could but once get rid of a few of their prejudices about the necessity of attending to business, I should not despair of their adopting the same plan; for it is from no distaste to music, nor yet want of performers, that glees are not sung on the Stock Exchange and quartetts played at Lloyd's Coffee-house; and I believe that, among many, scores and *shifting* are nearly as much the topics of discussion as prices and insurance.

The echo of the first blast of instruments from the flag-stone pavement across the wide market-place soon brings together a musical crowd for half an hour's enjoyment. The music, after a full overture or two, always concludes with a simple chorale, which, softly breathed from four trombones, produces one of the most delicate combinations I ever heard; and though a great part of the audience vanishes at its commencement, it " fit audience finds, though few." The merchants of Leipsic may the more readily acquiesce in this interruption to business after the severe lesson they have learned on the vanity of placing their affections on things below and terrestrial joys; from bullets sticking in their walls, the memory of contributions levied on them, and also of that time when they were obliged to entertain the military, they are led na-

turally to reflect on the instability of human pos-
sessions, and the wisdom of present enjoyment.
In no part of Germany can one procure a more
vivid idea of the horrors of war than in this city;
as I walked through one of the gates of it, accompanied by a kind German friend, " There," said
he, talking of the battle of Leipsic, and pointing
to a woman at work in a field, " stood the emperor,
in his tri-cornered hat,* looking perfectly uncon-
cerned, warming himself at a fire, and surrounded
by his aides-de-camp; in that farm-house he lodged;
here was I when the firing commenced. The English
people little know the misery it is to meet all one's
female friends and relations in a cellar, during such
times the only healthy part of one's house." From
the steeples of the churches at night the numerous
fires and signal rockets of the army without were
viewed with silence and shuddering. Many an
impending fate was then undecided, and a few days
were to settle what sacrifice of friends, or fortune,
or of person was to fall to the share of the spec-

* Napoleon's hat, which was lost in the hurry of the
battle of Waterloo, was picked up by a drummer, and is
now to be seen in the Museum of Berlin. Many of the
Prussians too well recollect the face it shaded, to wish for a
repetition of that view.

tator. This terrible event will not soon be erased from the memories of the Leipsic citizens.

I should not mention La Vestale of Spontini, which by the way is an opera admirably accompanied in Leipsic, were it not for the abominable system it exposes of overloading songs with as thick a score of instruments as might be found in a sinfonia or overture. This is the only excuse that singers can have for " tearing a passion to tatters," and "splitting the ears of the groundlings;" and it is a practice not only discountenanced by the greatest masters of effect, but contrary to the dictates of common reason and judgment. Parts of the second act of this opera make one regret that it should contain so heinous a fault, for there, some of the airs assume a very grand and heroic character. But why Julia should, with the consciousness of broken vows, and even the fear of death upon her, be called upon to overpower four horns and three trombones, is hard to guess. Weber is one of the moderns who has followed the noisy example, and it is a method which not only destroys the clearness of the parts, but robs the overture of its most striking peculiarity.

In St. Thomas's school, and under the direction of M. Weinlich, the resident professor and musical instructor, I heard a sacred cantata, called "Das Halleluja der Schöpfung," composed by Kunzen, a capell-meister, who died some years since in Copenhagen. This music was played by a full band and chorus, in a room not much larger than a drawing-room of moderate size, and as the *tutti* parts were " frequent and full," the noise would have astounded any one less seasoned to conservatorios and practice rooms than myself. Here was also tried, part of Eybler's Offertorium, a composition which has passed into the north of Europe with more good fortune than a close imitation of the common-places of Haydn's melody, and the operatic model of solos, accompanied by a chorus, deserves. Eybler might well take a lesson of honest master Schicht, who, as his choruses show, was a straight-forward contrapuntist, working out the subjects of his fugues in the true Handel and Graun fashion, without stoppage, let, or hinderance. The grand choral motetts used in the reformed service at Leipsic, which appear to have grown out of the simplicity of the *corale*, are as well worth hearing as any thing in the church music of Germany.

WEIMAR, EISENACH, &c.

WEIMAR is a spot where the muses love to " haunt clear spring and shady grove and sunny hill;" it is redolent of music and poetry, for here Hummel and Göthe reside, and the grand duke is well known as a Mæcenas, who draws around him the highest genius of his country. Here an affable and unostentatious court is kept up without its endless formalities; it seems a place of gardens and retired leisure, where among the wood nymphs, the turmoil of worldly ambition may give way to the calm of contemplation, and the enjoyment of poetic ease. The arrangement of the royal grounds and plantations, the design of bridges and fountains, announce the elegant and tasteful mind of the proprietor. The library, leading at once into sylvan glades; the pavilion in the interior of the grounds, which cheats the wanderer with the appearance of a Gothic chapel; the monuments and baths, all replete with classical association, either by means of sculpture or inscription, make this the spot for

" youthful poet's dream." For the luxurious idler
who chooses to throw away part of a sunny morning in watching the golden mouths and bellies of
the perch, which here, unharmed by Isaak Waltons
and impaling hooks, reveal themselves in sporting
on the surface of a stream, the garden is Elysian ;
not to mention the delights of a wilderness of pea-
cocks, besides many kinds of strange exotic fowl,
that " hop in his walks and gambol in his eyes."

But to leave rhapsodies on garden pleasures, and
to speak of the still more attractive union of amia-
bility and genius in the person of a human being,
I must turn to Hummel, the Apollo of this sacred
spot. This musician, who might be surnamed the
good, with as much justice as any person who ever
earned that appellation, shows how much unaffected
simplicity and friendly and caressing manners become one who is the musical idol of his countrymen; and upon whom " blushing honours " sit as
easily, and are worn as carelessly as his morning
robe. It is delightful to meet a great musician in
his *mental* undress, when he sits down to his pianoforte, and is liberal of what comes uppermost,
lavishing thoughts and beauties with a noble prodigality. Hummel is, I think, the most charming
and original *extemporiser* on the pianoforte that

exists, for the fertility of his mind and the volition of his ideas, which seem in their endless ramifications quite inexhaustible, I have never heard his equal. It was my good fortune to spend some hours with Hummel, and while he played, to trace with eager interest the treatment of every new idea and melodious passage, and never have I employed time with greater satisfaction. In such playing as Hummel's one may hear the orchestral writer and deep thinker, as well as the mere pianist; passages of difficult execution do not arise to show what he can do with his fingers, but because his hand performs what his head conceives, and that sometimes chooses the crooked instead of the straight path. The most exquisite peculiarity of Hummel's mind is its lovely flow of melody, the elegant phrases which constantly start up, which, though not to be anticipated by the hearer, are never far-fetched or extravagant. His gliding, smooth, and expressive style; the beauty of his touch, which combines force, crispness, and delicacy; the soul of his appogiature, and his refined modulation, are all true inheritances from Mozart. Hummel's performance is full and rich, and in the midst of all the modern polish of his melody those organic features with which his compositions abound, the imitations, fugued points, and sequences which enrich *extempore* playing, are not neglected. He is never lost in a fool's paradise in following a subject; but his eye, when I happened to catch it, showed an utter absence of sensation to external things in communing with the spirit of Beauty. Hummel told me, that he was so much engaged in composition, and in the superintendence of his opera, that he had little time for the pianoforte, and that he seldom played except when travelling; and in proof of what he said, showed me, laughing, his finger nails, which were grown into a very Nebuchadnezzar-like kind of longitude. This fact made his execution still more wonderful, as if a mere effort of the will were to ensure the hitting of distances, and the overcoming of mechanical difficulties. He was pleased to hear that a lady (Mrs. Anderson) had repeatedly played in public his septett for the pianoforte, and observed that to go through that piece required greater strength of hand than female performers generally possessed. We talked of the musical taste of Vienna, for which I found he had as little admiration as myself. It has been said that we become acquainted with the best part of an author in his writings, which saying has many exceptions to its truth, and in no person more especially than in Hummel. If there is any thing in physiognomy, in the tone of a voice, in hearty likings and as hearty dislikings, in honest sentiments, and true delicacy of mind, this great musician is fifty times more to be loved for himself than to be admired for his genius.

Erfurt, now a stout Prussian fortress, brimful of soldiers, is one of the most remarkable and interesting towns of Germany; it is exactly that which would answer to a young lady's idea of "a queer sort of place." After one has done wondering at the immense thickness and solidity of the walls, the attention is caught by the stately look of the houses, which, for the length of a street, are embellished with a fine frieze, "with bossy sculptures graven." What event the historian of these heroes in doublet and hose intended to commemorate, I must leave to the research of future travellers of more leisure as well as antiquarian knowledge.

The cathedral here is excessively battered, but it is admirably quaint in the devices of its tombs and ornaments. It stands on an eminence; three or four flights of delapidated steps lead to a ruined cloister, where the kitchen of the monks is yet palpable, and well begrimed it is with the smoke of their roast. The cathedral, though having perhaps

served for a stable to the French, as its companions have done, is a genuine remnant of " the
olden time." I visited this place about six o'clock
in the morning; an old priest was in one of the
lower chapels, busy in mumbling his matins to a
slender congregation of three—(the deep hollow
murmur of his voice had not a bad effect, and the
early sun streaming through the rich windows of a
cathedral was a sight to be enjoyed); grim colossal
figures in tapestry stood on one side the nave, and
that tough knight who won an extra wife in Pales-
tine looked out from between his two dames, in a
state of calmness with which we may suppose he was
little acquainted in his life-time. The small square
stones which pave this building lie as uneven as
the waves of the sea; the choir is crowded with
trophies of the crusades, and the banners of Tem-
plar knights. In the choir was a magnificent collection of Gregorian music, the only kind which
should co-exist with the rude antiquity of this
cathedral.

A travelling concert was given at Erfurt by the
music-director Eberwein, of Weimar, at which
every one present was much pleased. The manner
in which the German musician gets up one of these
performances (which, by the way, never wants

hearers) furnishes an illustration of the different natures of an English and German audience, the former only satisfied with a variety of names, the latter enduring but one for the whole length of a concert bill. The professor having collected his wife, children, aunts, nieces, &c. they jog off in company, and on arriving at some strange town, he writes an overture, his wife sings, his son plays a concerto on the violin, his daughter on the pianoforte, the rest do what they can, and they thus make up some of the prettiest family harmony imaginable.

On quitting Erfurt I resolved to pass Saxe Gotha, and make the best way I could to Eisenach. In this place I found a fine little green country village, comprising the most rural of inns, where eels are usually discussed by travellers, among other varieties of foison; the house was very quiet and comfortable, though his majesty of Bavaria, as I was informed, was dining in the next apartment. From the window of this inn there is a pleasant assemblage of objects in the distance for the enjoyment of any one who likes an Epicurean relish to his wine; first there is the fountain, surmounted with the antique statue of an armed knight; the old church, almost overshadowed by a grove of linden trees; the village school; and, in the back-ground, a craggy pine-clad mountain, Der Wartberg, crowned with the ancient castle of the landgraves of Thuringia. How old those titles seem! It is delightful to see how the Germans cherish the memory of their chivalry; that they cling to the remnants of the romance of their history so heartily, that there is not a single ruinous baronial castle among them that is not *repaired* into an excellent state of decay. One does not climb the precipitous and topling heights of Der Wartberg for the sake of a view, nor to employ the imagination in restoring apartments and inhabitants to bare walls, but to see a still habitable domain in some parts slightly restored, the same stony walls and long arched passages, which formed the impregnable lair of Louis the Iron and Dame Cunigonda. That Luther here took refuge in his troubles, inhabited a solitary prison-like apartment, here wrestled and prayed, or revolved his chances of martyrdom, give little pleasure; other more poetical subjects occupy the mind. To pass a stormy night in the eating hall of this place, which is hung round with moth-eaten portraits, in listening to stories of the old proprietors, by the side of a blazing hearth, would lap the soul of Mary Anne Radcliffe in Elysium. The castle is still full of the harness and accoutrements of knights, and the gaunt hard visages of the landgraves are still visible in some tattered paintings; but in the book of their faces one finds a blank; they are fellows who, at the present day, would have made good coal-heavers; nor does the face of the lady Agnes or the Lady Cunigonda own any " soft impeachment," but a haughtiness and disdain that must have frozen the desires of a presumptuous minstrel. When the portal of this castle was once closed, the feeling of security must have been delicious, the vantage ground being so satisfactory in case of attack, and the inheritor of such a tenement might almost apply to himself literally the noble meta-phor Shakespear has put in the mouth of Richard:

> " But I was born so high,
>   Our eyrie buildeth in the cedar's top,
>   And dallies with the wind, and scorns the sun."

On an opposite eminence to Der Wartberg, in the midst of a forest of pines, stands the ruin of a monastery, which it may be supposed was extremely convenient for the Lady Cunigonda, in the event of her committing any slight peccadillo which re-quired shrift. Legends are rife here of debauched monks, who were punished by special mission from heaven; and really the choice of situation seems

more like the entrenchment of a set of lawless
voluptuaries than of poor eremites and ascetics;
and the various passages and outlets from the
monastery, of which the stairs, hewn out of the
solid rock, must have cost incredible labour, the
mysterious and inscrutable holes which still bear
witness to the ingenuity of the founders, help to
encourage this opinion. Two tall fragments of
rock, which appear to have been riven in some con-
vulsion of the elements, and stand leaning together,
forming part of a natural arch, the common people
look at with this solemn investment; they say "they
represent the microcosms of a friar and his be-
loved, who, for one wicked kiss, well and heartily
twanged off, have undergone this cruel transub-
stantiation." I did not find that the contemplation
of this object had put such little amenities of behaviour out of fashion in Eisenach. I ascended to
this ruin alone on a damp and *drizzling* morning,
creeping tenderly through alleys of low firs or
pines, which were surcharged with water, and
ready upon the least violence to rain vengeance
upon the wayfarer; the castle of Wartberg and
the highest trees about it were enveloped in mist,
and a thick steam was ascending in twenty places
from that green forest; from the summit nature

looked well, nor did the thought of those " ugly customers," wild boars, of which the breed is here not quite exterminated, allow the fancy to sleep. None but a Dutchman, phlegmatic and unimpassioned (as that one who is related, on the authority of a Moravian minister, to have fought a tiger foot to foot at the Cape of Good Hope, and to have made his enemy sheer off), could have passed one of these European jungles without expecting to hear the grunt, and presently to see peering through the bushes, the red eyes, bristly head, white tusks, and fearful snout of one of the terrible originals of Schneider's paintings.

Long since the defunct landgraves of Thuringia have been forgotten, Eisenach has been rendered more famous by the production of John Sebastian Bach, whose family, as I was informed by a relative, was originally Hungarian, but was driven from its patrimony in the wars for religion. My informant, who traced his descent at two removes from Ernest, the brother of Sebastian, was the only one of the *auld* original stock left in the town, and he seemed not a little proud of his relationship, and was pleasingly elaborate and erudite in his disquisitions upon the science; although only a dilettante in music, his more serious occupation being that of a clerk or writer, the lucky accident of his birth has been to him a fortune of smiling thoughts. I found in this individual a good specimen of the simple, unostentatious, yet well-informed German; our interview took place in the open air, where he, not inconvenienced by holding under his arm an immense bundle of official papers, leaned quietly against a buttress of the old church, and discoursed of music from the first grand discoveries made by his great uncle, down to the most transient productions of the day, to my great content, and the edification of the village organist. Nature has made a little mistake in choosing this pretty country town to forge such a masterpiece of her workmanship as Bach; he should have been the born king of the Terra del Fuego, if we may imagine a Utopia where all the subjects are fugues. That Bach was the absolute monarch of his *subjects* is not to be denied. No traces of his organ-playing, or anecdotes of his compositions, are to be found here, Sebastian Bach having early pitched his residence in Leipsic.

The church of this place, which I have mentioned, might, from its want of a tower or steeple, be taken for a huge stable; it contains a large, worn-out old organ, at which, during the Lutheran service, the player laboured in vain. The keys were pressed down to no purpose, the pedals refused to answer, in vain were the bellows duly and diligently worked by two men; the choir was as much too young as the instrument too old, and the chorales as bad in their effect as might be desired.

I should like to have sung, if I had been able, the epithalamium of a young couple, who, in company with their friends and a venerable-looking clergyman, issued forth from the church one bright morning in a nuptial procession; it was a sight which looked especially graceful in a rural place, where the vices of cities have made no inroad, and people have not learned to be ashamed of the best parts of their nature. The whole party walked with uncovered heads, the bride stepped first with a modest dignity in her demeanour, " grave with glad thoughts," and seemed so familiar with her situation, that she must have been born with a genius for the conjugal state. Last came the " new abashed " husband, who appeared painfully conscious of his honours, and the only one of the whole train who was ill at ease. This little matrimonial parade looked more like the first innocence and the simple spirit of the contract than the guilty stealth with which the fact of marriage is

perpetrated among us.—The journey to Cassel is
performed over hideous roads, but through a country which looks like one long orchard; hill and
dale, forest scenery, or rich pasture, by turns vary
the loveliness of the prospect. In the villages of
the Hessian dominions, the inhabitants, with all
their wealth of live stock as farmers, live in dirt
and squalor: the rafters over the doors of their
dwellings are sooty with the smoke which escapes
from the principal entrance; pigs are advanced to
the dignity of parlour-boarders; a hay-stack is the
bosom friend of the master and his family. Inscriptions notched in the door-ways, so as to be
easily read and remembered, are pregnant with reflection for the moralist; some pious, for the ad-
monition and virtuous nurture of children; others
inculcating the rewards of diligence for servants;
others, more romantic and less sinister, running in
Latin thus—" Johannes Flügel et Uxor Anna
Christina, 1811." If Johannes is in the field at
plough, what does the reader think is the elegant
employment of his chaste Lucretia? Not spinning
among her maids at home; but it is more than probable that the lovely Anna Christina, with a good
stick in her hand, and with more speed than the
Gryphon pursued the Arimaspian, *spins* down a

plashy lane, after a volatile hog, or goose not to be consoled, " that swims, or sinks, or wades, or creeps, or flies." This incongruous name for the wife of a peasant is only one out of a collection of very amusing curiosities to be read by any traveller between Eisenach and Cassel.

In this quarter of Germany the country people have no briskness and intelligence in their looks, but appear as stupid as the beasts they domesticate, and more surly. At a little hedge inn on this route, the haven of thirsty drivers and hungry horses, the master's daughter, a perfect Maritornes in dress and figure, and the Hebe of postillions and dragoons, was a pianoforte player. What time she could gain from the dispensing of *schnaps*,* she snatched a grace out of Cramer's lessons. Human nature never appeared in a more fantastic shape than it did in the person of her sire. He was the Olympian Jupiter of a dunghill, and had more disdain and hauteur on his countenance than if he had been nabob of Arcot; he stood with folded arms, and contemplated his possession of a yard full of mud, an empty stable, and a dozen ducks, with a dread frown of importance. He scorned civility to strangers, and

* A kind of dram.

had no idea of returning a bow; seeing which, some of my companions were waggishly profuse of respect. It would be hard for a novelist to draw such a caricature of mankind that the original should not be found between this and Tobolsk.

The *Lohn Kutcher* of Germany is more servile and obsequious in his conduct than the light-hearted and disinterested postillion; the former has an eye to his trink-geld, with which he has learned, like his fraternity in England, never to be satisfied, but his dissatisfaction never leads him beyond a gentle remonstrance with the " guter herr." One of those whom we hired sat brooding over our luggage, and from the fear of dirtying it, had placed his legs in such an unnatural state of distension, that we feared for the location of his hip-joints; a little more and the divorce would have been as complete as ever was achieved by the clown in a pantomime. When he had paid the toll-money at a barrier, he took leave of the people with an " Adieu " more mincingly pronounced, the *u* more " beautifully less," than it could have left the mouth of a fine lady; and having mounted and elongated his inferior limbs in opposite directions, he pronounced the mysterious word " Hicks," which never failed to terrify the horses into a motion. We became so accustomed to the repetition of "Adieu," " Hicks," that at last we began to fancy it the farewell of some pathetic Englishman.

Cassel, viewed from the road in the light of the setting sun, looks like a city of palaces in a fairy tale, " with glistering spires and pinnacles adorned." It is surrounded by fine bosky hills. Beautiful as the situation is, and cheap as is the expense of entertainment, there is no city in Germany in which I should less like to reside than Cassel ; the military swarm in this place, and there is such an eternal manœuvring and drumming going forward from morning to night, that the town is like one great barrack.

The theatre is inconsiderable, and it being engaged with the bad music of a French opera, I was induced to shorten my stay. A peculiarity in the orchestra of this theatre was, that it was half filled with officers, who *fiddled* in their regimental uniform without considering it derogatory to the dignity of their profession. This sight reminded me of the accomplishment of that blessed time foretold in the Scriptures, when " swords shall be turned into ploughshares."

Spohr, who sequesters himself among the green woods of Cassel, has an excellent band to write

for, and one of the best clarionet players I have
heard. The playing of this great *singer* on the
violin is too fresh in the recollection of the musical amateurs in England to render any particular
account of its characteristics a matter of interest;
it may be said, however, that though he plays less
than formerly, being much engaged in composition,
that his taste seems, if possible, heightened. A
young lady here one evening sang with great effect a
scena ed aria of Spohr, " Tu m' abbandoni, ingrato,"
which, for its excellence and purely *vocal* character, deserves to be generally known. It is a
piece of concert music, modelled on the grandest
plan of dramatic song, and consists of three movements—an introductory recitative accompanied,
an elegant *cantabile,* and an allegro in the *agitato*
style, full of energy and passion. All the writings
of the author of Faust are stamped with thought
and invention very much unlike ephemeral compositions, and what faults he has are so completely
overbalanced by the fertility and grace of his melodies, that he must rank among the first creative
geniuses of the age.

The German composer has these little advantages in his favour, that he lives in a country
where neither the estimate of a man's ability nor

the security of his prospects is affected by the state of his coat or pantaloons, nor is he compelled to slave for means to appear that which for its own sake he does not wish to appear. A great musician might walk out here, if he chose, clothed in drugget, and no one would think of him with the less respect, for his works have invested him with a perpetual dignity. The lesson-giving business of professors in England is the death-blow to their invention; and I can only compare the state of one of these, who, mewed to his drudgery, looks at a distance upon the heaven of a thoughtful leisure for ever out of his reach, to that of an old eagle chained, who year after year strains his eyes towards the sun, to which he may never again aspire.

In the Catholic church of Cassel the service is but indifferently performed; it is the only one in Germany that I have seen where high mass takes place to the accompaniment of a wretched organ. There is a vast difference between the immunities allowed to the canine species in Flanders and Germany; in the latter place the dogs run in and out of the churches, and clear up their little theological scruples as they choose, but in the former there is this intolerant mandate posted at the doors, " Honden oyt Godts Tempel."* While I attended mass one Sunday morning in Cassel, a large poodle, who had made his way into the gallery, on the commencement of the Kyrie elieson, was seized with such a fit of vocal inspiration, that, stretching out his neck and jaws, and turning his face upwards, he began to utter tones less mellifluous than loud; but the beadle soon interfered with this uncalled-for display of his *portamento*, by assisting him down stairs with his foot. There is a magnificent band of military instruments to be heard on Sundays in Cassel.

I pushed on from here to Amsterdam without making any considerable halt in any other town of pleasant Germany, to which the contrast of Holland appeared dreary beyond imagination. In journeying through this country the peasantry no longer attract notice by a well-chosen dress; the women, not embrowned like the German, and looking as if they had the wholesome smell of the fields upon them, but their heads all *becapped*, appear like round bundles of something.

It was on a very warm and wet Sunday that I had the first taste of the delights of Dutch scenery and a Dutch atmosphere, driving along a road as

* Dogs to be kept out of God's temple.

smooth as a carpetted drawing-room, occasionally embellished with straight rows of stunted poplars, and bounded by a canal on one side, and a ditch on the other. There was no getting out of sight of water. In the vicinity of Amsterdam the ostentatious country residences of the city merchants thrust themselves upon the notice; and, as though the cockney idea of rurality had sailed here, in the lodge, at the entrance of his grounds, sat the wealthy burger, with his powdered head and red face, spending his Sunday afternoon in smoking, revolving his affairs and looking at the stage-coaches, while his wife and daughters in the same room were melancholy over their tea ; to complete the fascination and salubrity of this apartment, a stagnant pool, with an appropriate " green mantle," lay under the windows. Money in Holland cannot procure absolute comfort, but only a mitigation of wretchedness ; it is a place in which, as some satirist has said, one goes " *on board.*" The cigars, chafing-dishes, and dram-bottles with which the inhabitants, who are ever foining with the ague, parry its thrusts, are to a stranger more intolerable than the damp air against which they are thought antidotes.

The Dutch may be equally wise and flower-loving, but they are neither handsome nor agreeable; their conversation is as lumbering as their language and formation.—There is no German opera at present in Amsterdam, the death of the principal singers having put a stop to it. At the Dutch theatre the audience is not select; whistling, hallooing, and fighting, absolutely unknown in German play-houses, flourish there.

Among some of the ladies here I found that fashion still existing in which the belles of Charles the Second's court are handed down to us, of covering the forehead with a row of delicate ringlets; and though this is a mode which appears to many to spoil a fine face, it may really be seen upon the living figure with less abomination.—Those who can imagine the *Hoog Duitsch* as the language of tenderness and amorous parle, may enjoy the dramatic exhibitions of the Dutch.

I bid farewell to good music in the performance of M. Herder and his sister, German artists, who were giving concerts in Amsterdam : their tour in Holland had been particularly successful, for their musical *soirées* were always crowded. The brother was a fine pianoforte player, but a still better composer : the sister was a soprano of the very first

class. M. Herder played a pianoforte quintett in
E flat of his composition, which might have be-
longed to Beethoven, and showed much quickness
in varying *extempore* themes which were handed to
him; and I noticed particularly a little air of
Fesca, which he adorned with great fancy and
feeling. They performed together the celebrated
cantata of Mozart, with pianoforte obligato, entitled "Non temer;" and the lady sang some airs
of the school of Hasse, and of an old oratorio of
Haydn, in a very sensible and delightful manner.
These performers, whom I met in private, entertained me with an account of the great progress of
music in Russia, from whence they have not long
returned.

Instrumental performance and composition are
cultivated so successfully at St. Petersburg, that
there is little prospect of patronage for any
musician who travels there without carrying
with him the highest accomplishments in his art;
but there is hardly any place where real talent is
better rewarded. The Russians are no longer a
horde of barbarians, to be satisfied with any thing;
and they are too industrious and clever in music
themselves not to be able to judge of the same qua-

lities in other people.—There are many fine professors of whom in England we know nothing, who
spend their summers either in Paris, or St. Petersburg, or Berlin, because they not only find patronage at these cities, but the expense of travelling
does not swallow up the whole profits of their tour:
they are enabled to save something to spend as
they like.   Many a German musician would be
glad to make a journey to London if he thought he
could *regain* his home from this expensive country,
and meet his family and friends a little richer than
he set out.   He has no idea of the felicity of being
caressed at the dinner-tables of great people for the
sake of his playing, and of seeing the music desks
make their appearance with the dessert.   A distinguished German composer observed to me, " I do
not want splendid entertainments when I go to
London—I can eat my dinner at home."   The
thought of being exhibited as a show among a
party of strangers of whom he knows nothing, is
repulsive to the pride of genius: if he must do
what is disagreeable to him, it would be, not for
the sake of hearing compliments or drinking fine
wines, but to gain some assistance against the time
when his fingers lose their elasticity, and his brain
gets dry.

No artists can be less mercenary in the exercise of their profession, none more ready to play for the pleasure of their friends, than the great musicians of Germany; but they have no skill in flattering the great, and no appetite for worthless praise. Most of them enjoy that enviable competency which enables them to pursue fame at their leisure; the little duties of their employment, such as directing an orchestra, or composing a few pieces for the entertainment of the nobleman of whose establishment they are part, are so easily discharged, as to leave them plenty of time for idleness if it was their taste to indulge in it. But this is not the case; they have " that last infirmity of noble minds," an appetite for fame, and labour as hard for the mere pleasure of inventing and combining as others do for the vulgar acquisition of wealth.

The ennobling power of the divine art of music is best felt where among a number of professors each strives to penetrate the deepest into its mysteries without envy and without sordid interest; and I believe it is the advantageous equality upon which they all start in pursuit of their favourite science which makes them liberal and ingenuous in the appreciation of contemporary talent. Until men of genius in other countries are placed out of the reach of vulgar wants or the fear of poverty, there can be no competition in any part of Europe with the musicians of Germany.

I have not thought it necessary to detail at length the little particulars of my journey homewards—how that I repassed into Flanders, and shipped myself on board the good ship The Superb, Captain H. Stranack, bound from Ostend to the Tower Wharf—and how this little book had like to have been lost to the world by the unceremonious behaviour of a barge, which nearly overran the boat that carried its author ashore, unless, like Cæsar, he had swam to land with his Commentaries in his mouth. Fortunately this unexpected cadence did not take place; as nothing was more remote from the writer's intentions than swimming, so was nothing less suited than his dress for committing himself to the flood; for even Cæsar himself, had he been wrapped in a huge travelling cloak, with a cap flapped over his ears, wearing a thick pair of boots, and having his pockets stuffed with music, might have found the evolutions of his legs and hands not quite

so satisfactory as thirty feet of water might induce him to wish. Whether the reader may
consider the escape matter of congratulation remains to be proved.

THE END.

INDEXES

INDEX OF PERSONS AND PLACES

INDEX OF MUSIC MENTIONED
IN THE TEXT

295